UT UNUM SINT: STUDIES ON PAPAL PRIMACY

THE REFORM

OF THE

PAPACY

THE COSTLY CALL
TO CHRISTIAN UNITY

JOHN R. QUINN

A Herder and Herder Book
The Crossroad Publishing Company
New York

The Crossroad Publishing Company
370 Lexington Avenue, New York, NY 10017

Printed in the United States of America

Library of Congress Cataloging-in-Publication Data

Quinn, John R. (John Raphael), 1929–
    The reform of the papacy : the costly call to Christian unity /
John R. Quinn.
        p.   cm.
    Includes bibliographical references.
    ISBN 0-8245-1826-8
    1. Popes—Primacy.   2. Petrine office.   3. Papacy and
Christian union.   I. Title.
BX1805.Q56   1999
262'.13—dc21   99-38951
                                                            CIP

1   2   3   4   5   6   7   8   9   10   03   02   01   00   99

To my parents,
who loved the Church,
my first teachers and examples of faith

and to

Vincent A. McCormick, S.J.
and
Edward J. Malatesta, S.J.

and to

The Society of Jesus,
a singular and providential gift
of the Heart of Christ
to the Church

Contents

Preface

This book is one bishop's attempt to respond to Pope John Paul II's request for bishops to engage with him in a patient and fraternal dialogue about the papacy.[1] Specifically, the pope initiates a dialogue aimed at the reform of the papacy whereby it could become more a "service of love recognized by all concerned" (*Ut unum sint* §95). He is clearly aware, and says so explicitly, that the papal ministry as it now exists constitutes something of an obstacle to Christian unity (ibid. §88). It is with a great desire to remove the obstacle that the Pope asks for a dialogue on the papacy.

In a sense, then, this book is not my idea. It is the Pope himself who has opened the question of the papacy in his landmark encyclical on Christian unity. It is the Pope himself who has asked bishops to respond. In chapter 1, I treat more fully what the Pope says in that encyclical.

This book is written at what Karl Rahner has called the first level of reflection. It is not the work of a professional theologian who has spent his life in study, research, and teaching. While it makes use of theology and history, it is more the reflections of a bishop which may need to be corrected, modified, augmented, or confirmed by the work of theologians and scholars, as well as by my brother bishops.

It should be obvious that I profess the Church's ever new

[1] Pope John Paul II, Encyclical Letter on Commitment to Ecumenism, *Ut unum sint*, May 25, 1995, §95.

9

and ever ancient faith concerning the primacy of Peter and his successors. Without that faith this book would never have been written. At the same time, I also recognize the accepted Catholic teaching about the development of doctrine, nowhere more fully or compellingly set forth than in Cardinal Newman's "An Essay on the Development of Christian Doctrine."[2] The Petrine office, like all other doctrines of the faith, has undergone development. Among these doctrines are the mystery of the Trinity, the Incarnation, the creed, the canon of scripture—and the primacy of the Pope as Successor of Peter. If doctrinal development is not understood and assumed as an established principle in the Church, *Ut unum sint* and my effort to respond to it could never have been written.

The Pope has raised a question. The dignity of his office, his personal integrity, and the crucial nature of the question demand an honest response. To speak of new ways of exercising the primacy is necessarily to criticize past and present ways of its exercise as inadequate. Honesty can be painful. My goal is "to speak the truth in love." I state once again what I have said before: "I speak completely in fidelity to the Church, One and Catholic. Indeed, in the Second Vatican Council many cardinals and bishops said much of what I have said here. . . ."[3]

I could not have written this book alone. Here I want to express my gratitude to the Catholic, Orthdox, and Anglican scholars, to the bishops and Catholic lay men and women who have read the manuscript and made valued and positive contributions to the work and directed me to sources I am not likely otherwise to have discovered.

---

[2] John Henry Newman, *An Essay on the Development of Christian Doctrine* (Westminster, Md.: Christian Classics, 1968).

[3] John R. Quinn, "The Exercise of the Primacy" (lecture delivered on the occasion of the centenary of Campion Hall, Oxford, June 29, 1996, published in *Commonweal*, July 12, 1996).

My final thought. This book, like most others, will provoke both positive and negative reactions. I am grateful for both because it is my desire to emulate the example of Thomas Aquinas, who, following the custom of the great theologians of his time, submitted all his work to "better judgment," *salvo meliori iudicio.*

Augustine, too, experienced praise and censure for his work. In the third chapter of his great work on the Trinity, he provides words with which I can introduce this work:

> The reader who takes up my book and says, "This is not said well" . . . attacks my language not my faith. . . . Indeed, it could perhaps have been done better. Even so, no human being has ever spoken in such a way that he could be understood on every point by everyone. If a reader should not like my book, he should set it aside or even throw it away. . . . It is helpful, then, to have diverse writers but not diverse faith.

CHAPTER 1

The Encyclical Ut Unum Sint: The Papacy and Christian Unity

Revolution is not necessarily violent or negative. The discovery of radium by Madame Curie was a revolution in medicine and a signal benefit to humanity. Even so, revolution does not readily come to mind when we think of the papacy. Yet the Second Vatican Council called by Pope John XXIII was in the best sense a revolution, setting the Church on a new trajectory and profoundly touching all aspects of her life. It was a transformation expressed in terms of opening the windows, letting in fresh air and new light. The opening of the windows and the new light enabled the Church to see her own internal life in a new way, its strengths and weaknesses, its fidelities and infidelities. Open windows also made it possible for the Church to look out and see beyond itself, to see the world with its joys and hopes, its promise, its contradictions, its torments, and its tragedies. The new vision fashioned by the council called the Church to bear the image of its Lord, who came not only to serve but, more radically, to lay down his life for others. The council called the Church to witness more clearly its communion with the folly of the cross by a more evident poverty, by an evident humility and by an evident and unselfish love.

In a similar way, the encyclical[1] letter of Pope John Paul II

---

[1] An encyclical is a papal letter addressed usually to the world episcopate. Some have a wider designation: to bishops, lay Catholics, and all men and women of good will. This particular encyclical, dated May 25, 1995, and published by Libreria Editrice Vaticana, Vatican City, is unique

on Christian unity, entitled *Ut unum sint* (That they may be one), must also be called a revolution. For the first time it is the Pope himself who raises and legitimizes the question of reform and change in the papal office in the Church. Pope John Paul II calls for a widespread discussion of how this reform could be brought about and what shape it could take.

The encyclical has elicited some serious and thoughtful responses. The distinguished Orthodox theologian Olivier Clément, has written a challenging work entitled *Rome autrement,* which I translate as "A Different Rome."[2] Hermann J. Pottmeyer has published *Towards a Papacy in Communion* in response to the encyclical, a carefully reasoned and important contribution to the discussion of a reform of the papacy.[3] The Church of England has also presented a formal response to the encyclical.[4] In the fall of 1996, the Congregation for the Doctrine of the Faith sponsored a symposium on the primacy of the Successor of Peter.[5] Yet notwithstanding these and other responses, the radical and precedent-breaking character of the encyclical has not been fully appreciated, nor has it attracted the wider interest its truly daring invitation and declarations merit.

In a departure from custom, for instance, the letter is not addressed to any specific group or nation. The Pope does not speak of himself as the "Holy Father" or as the "Vicar of

---

in that no audience is specifically designated, implying that it is addressed to all persons of good will. The word "encyclical" means that it is a letter to be circulated. References to sections of this encyclical throughout this book will use the abbreviation *UUS.*

[2] Olivier Clément, *Rome autrement* (Paris: Desclée de Brouwer, 1997).

[3] Hermann J. Pottmeyer, *Towards a Papacy in Communion* (New York: Crossroad, 1998).

[4] *That They All May Be One* (London: Church House Publishing, 1997).

[5] The papers given at this symposium have been published in *Il primato del successore di Pietro: Atti del simposio teologico, Roma, dicembre 1996* (Vatican City: Libreria Editrice Vaticana, 1997). One paper given at this symposium has been published in English: Michael J. Buckley, S.J., *Papal Primacy and the Episcopate* (New York: Crossroad, 1998).

Christ" but uses terms of greater simplicity such as "Bishop of Rome," "Successor of Peter," and "Servant of the Servants of God."[6] He admits the paradox that "the Catholic Church's conviction that in the ministry of the Bishop of Rome she has preserved . . . the visible sign and guarantor of unity, constitutes a difficulty for most other Christians" (*UUS* §88). The Pope experiences a special need to respond to this problem:

> I am convinced that I have a particular responsibility . . . above all in acknowledging the ecumenical aspirations of the majority of the Christian Communities and in heeding the request made of me to find a way of exercising the primacy which, while in no way renouncing what is essential to its mission, is nonetheless open to a new situation. (*UUS* §95)

The Pope further admits his own inability to carry out the task without help: "This is an immense task, which we cannot refuse and which I cannot carry out by myself" (*UUS* §96). This is a declaration that the Pope does not have the answer himself—he does not have a ready-made, take-it-or-leave-it solution.

Why the Invitation to Look at the Papacy?

Why are the reform of the papacy and the search for unity so important? Because, as the Pope points out, division among Christians is the enemy of the gospel.

> When non-believers meet missionaries who do not agree among themselves, even though they all appeal to Christ, will they be in a position to receive the true message? Will they not think that the Gospel is a cause of division, despite the fact that it is presented as the fundamental law of love? (*UUS* §98)

---

[6] The title Vicar of Christ, as Vatican II noted, belongs to all bishops; see *Lumen Gentium* (Dogmatic Constitution on the Church) §27. Throughout this book this document is cited according to *Decrees of the Ecumenical Councils,* ed. Norman P. Tanner, S.J., 2 vols. (New York: Sheed & Ward; Washington, D.C.: Georgetown University Press, 1990),

While there is division among Christians, the Church cannot adequately fulfill its mission in the world. The non-Christian, not only in distant lands but in our sophisticated industrial societies, is deterred by the mutual censures and condemnations of one Christian Church by another and by mutually contradictory doctrines. The Pope asks the penetrating question,

> How could (believers) refuse to do everything possible, with God's help, to break down the walls of division and distrust, to overcome obstacles and prejudices which thwart the proclamation of the Gospel of salvation in the Cross of Jesus . . . ? (*UUS* §2)

There is an urgency to the pursuit of unity and to finding a new way of exercising the primacy not only because disunity is so destructive but above all because our lack of unity is so clearly contrary to the will of Christ. The words of Christ, words that are a continuing indictment, should sting the conscience of every thoughtful believer: "Holy Father, protect them in your name that you have given me, so that they may be one, as we are one" (John 17:11). The desire to do the will of Christ must be the basic motive that gives new energy to the genuine and courageous search for a renewed primacy and for unity. The continuing search for the will of God, after all, is a fundamental mark of discipleship as it is the driving force of Jesus' life. "I have come not to do my own will but the will of him who sent me" (John 17:11). And he instructs his followers to make their daily prayer: "Thy kingdom come, Thy will be done on earth as it is in heaven" (Matt. 6:9–10).

The Pope is issuing this invitation to look at the papacy because the unity of Christians is at the heart of the Church's mission.

2:849–98. Another title by which the Popes were designated in past times and which is still used in the Mass for a deceased Pope is Vicar of Peter, which was the favored title of Gregory VII. See H. E. J. Cowdrey, *Pope Gregory VII* (Oxford: Clarendon Press, 1998), 525.

This unity, which the Lord has bestowed on his Church, and in which he wishes to embrace all people is not something added on, but stands at the very heart of Christ's mission. Nor is it some secondary attribute of the community of his disciples. Rather, it belongs to the very essence of this community. . . .

Thus it is absolutely clear that ecumenism, the movement promoting Christian unity, *is not just some sort of "appendix"* which is added to the Church's traditional activity. Rather, ecumenism is an organic part of her life and work, and consequently must pervade all that she is and does. . . . (*UUS* §§9, 20)

The search for unity must pervade the whole life of the Church. This is another example of the revolutionary character of this encyclical. Until the Second Vatican Council, ecumenism was regarded as dangerous to faith, and only tried and true experts engaged in it very cautiously, if at all. Here the Pope is saying that it must pervade everything in the Church.

The Cross, Prayer, and Conversion

How does the Pope propose to pursue the search for unity? At the outset, he mentions four things: the centrality of the cross, reflection, prayer, and conversion (*UUS* §7).[7] There must be honest reflection on past differences, the purification of memories, mutual forgiveness, and an honest, clear, and calm vision of the present divisions.

None of these dispositions of the heart is possible without a contemplative vision of the cross of Christ. The cross is the Tree of Life. But there is a certain, perhaps unconscious, level of unbelief even among Christians. Many of us want the gospel more eagerly than the cross. Yet the mature disciple has learned that Christ crucified is "the power of God and the wisdom of God" (1 Cor. 1:24). Christian unity will

---

[7] For an excellent treatment of the need for purity of heart and intention in such matters, see Buckley, *Papal Primacy,* 27–31.

not be accomplished by human power or human cleverness alone. It will be accomplished only by the poverty and humility of the cross. The Christian who truly seeks unity must embrace the cross. In this context the whole Church could fittingly recall Augustine's teaching about the magisterium of the cross,[8] the great school of Christian unity and reconciliation.

If the achievement of Christian unity is rooted in the cross, it cannot be accomplished without prayer for personal conversion. Another sign of the revolutionary character of this encyclical are these words of the Pope:

> This is a specific duty of the Bishop of Rome. . . . I carry out this duty [i.e., the search for unity] with the profound conviction that I am obeying the Lord, and with a clear sense of my own human frailty. (*UUS* §§3–4)

This is no perfunctory admission. Cardinal Newman has pointed out: "[S]elf-knowledge is at the root of all real religious knowledge. . . . God speaks to us primarily in our hearts. Self-knowledge is the key to the precepts and the doctrines of Scripture."[9] The Pope then goes on to speak of his own need for personal conversion and asks the whole Church to pray for it:

> The Bishop of Rome himself must fervently make his own Christ's prayer for that conversion which is indispensable for "Peter" to be able to serve his brethren. I earnestly invite the faithful of the Catholic Church and all Christians to share in

---

[8] Augustine, *Sermon* 315.1–2, 8 (in *Patrologiae cursus completus: Series latina,* ed. J. P. Migne, 221 vols. [Paris, 1844–64], vol. 38 [hereafter *PL*]). Speaking of the martyrdom of St. Stephen, Augustine recalls Stephen's prayer at the moment of his death, "Father, do not hold this sin against them," and how this was like the prayer of Jesus on the cross, "Father forgive them, for they know not what they do." He then observes, "He sat on the chair of the Cross and taught Stephen the law of holiness" (Sedebat in cathedra crucis et docebat Stephanum regulam pietatis).

[9] John Henry Newman, *Parochial and Plain Sermons,* vol. 1, *Secret Faults* (Westminster, Md.: Christian Classics, 1966), 42–43.

this prayer. May all join me in praying for this conversion!
(*UUS* §4)

This is an astonishing request. What if all over the world Christians prayed for the conversion of the Pope? What if such a prayer took place in Rome itself—at the tombs of the apostles Peter and Paul? Yet the Pope is clearly asking all to pray for his conversion. What if the Patriarch of Constantinople and the Archbishop of Canterbury and the World Council of Churches prayed for, and asked all Christians to pray for, their conversion? Startling advances might occur in the quest for Christian unity because the seekers would all be walking together the path of humility acknowledging that "all have sinned and fall short of the glory of God" (Rom. 3:23).

Unity springs from the silent prayer of communion with God, but also from the shared prayer of brothers and sisters. "Along the path to unity, pride of place certainly belongs to common prayer, the prayerful union of those who gather together around Christ himself" (*UUS* §22). Prayer is a witness that unity is not so much the fruit of human effort as it is the gift of Christ. "Peace I leave with you; my peace I give you. I do not give to you as the world gives" (John 14:27). It is prayer that disposes the hearts of believers to receive the gift of peace and unity. Prayer, common prayer, is a condition and context for the fraternal dialogue.

Anglican Robert Macfarlane comments:

> Placing John Paul's commitment to objective truth in relationship with prayer, common prayer with ecumenical partners, and with dialog, one can imagine an intense, at times vexing, but potentially creative tension that could produce results unexpected by anyone. Together prayer and dialog may be the trojan horse that releases in our midst such quietly splendid truth as none of us might have imagined.[10]

---

[10] Robert Macfarlane, "An Anglican Response to the Encyclical, *Ut Unum Sint*," *Ecumenical Trends* 25 (January 1996): 12.

Yet another reason why prayer is a crucial element of the fraternal dialogue is that Christian unity will exact a price. It will require the willingness to sacrifice. Prayer shapes and purifies the heart for the great things God asks. There must be not only a search and a strategy; there must be a spirituality of Christian unity.

It would be illusory for Catholics to think of the search for unity as a dynamic in which the Orthodox and Protestants make various changes and establish full communion with the Catholic Church, while the Catholic Church remains unchanged in every respect. We have to face the fact that in the service of Christian unity, the Catholic Church will have to make significant structural, pastoral, and canonical changes. Collegiality, participation of the laity, decentralization, and greater openness to diversity are some obvious areas where the Catholic Church will have to make changes.

Paolo Ricca, a Waldensian scholar,[11] responding to *Ut unum sint,* signals that unity will demand more than superficial measures:

> John Paul II undoubtedly has at heart the cause of Christian unity, of whose necessity and urgency he must be ever more convinced. . . . He must be convinced that the papacy as it is today has no real ecumenical chance. To have one, it must change.[12]

---

[11] The Waldensians originated early in the thirteenth century, before the Protestant Reformation. At the time of the Reformation a segment simply became Protestant. Another segment, particularly in Italy, retained their original identity and today are known as the "Chiesa Evangelica Valdese," the Evangelical Waldensian Church. They have a theological college in Rome. At least one of their churches in Rome, located about halfway between the Angelicum (the Dominicans) and the Gregorian University (the Jesuits), bears over its entrance the words of John's Gospel, *Lux lucet in tenebris,* "the light shines in the darkness." See *The Oxford Dictionary of the Christian Church,* ed. F. L. Cross and E. A. Livingstone (New York: Oxford University Press, 1997), 1714–15.

[12] Paolo Ricca, "The Papacy in Discussion: Expectations and Perspectives for the Third Millennium," *One in Christ* 33, no. 4 (1997): 283.

Unity will exact a price. It will not be won by cosmetic changes.

Dialogue and the Search for Unity

The contemplative vision of the cross, together with reflection, prayer, and conversion of heart, prepares the way for dialogue. In fact, some two-thirds of *Ut unum sint* is concerned with prayer and dialogue. Of dialogue the Pope says, "Dialog has not only been undertaken; *it has become an outright necessity, one of the Church's priorities*" (*UUS* §31).[13]

Dialogue is not conflict, an effort to prove oneself right and the other wrong. It is not carried out in hostility or hauteur: "It is necessary to pass from antagonism and conflict to a situation where each party recognizes the other as a *partner* . . . any display of mutual opposition must disappear" (*UUS* §29). Dialogue is peaceful, hopeful, without anger, and respectful. Its tone is earnest, humble, friendly, and searching.

This unity is not achieved by coercion, argument, or ultimatums. It is carried on with freedom and in mutual respect. The Pope says:

> As the Council's Declaration on Religious Freedom affirms, "Truth is to be sought after in a manner proper to the dignity of the human person and his social nature. The inquiry is to be free, carried on with the aid of teaching or instruction, communication, and dialog." . . . Ecumenical dialog is of essential importance. . . . (*UUS* §32).

Against this background, addressing the Patriarch of Constantinople in St. Peter's Basilica, the Pope says:

> I insistently pray the Holy Spirit to shine his light upon us, enlightening all the Pastors and theologians of our Churches, that we may seek—together, of course—the forms in which

---

[13] There is an extensive treatment of dialogue in §§28–39 of the encyclical.

this ministry may accomplish a service of love recognized by all concerned. (*UUS* §95)

The first seekers of a new way of exercising the primacy are the bishops and theologians of the Orthodox and Catholic Churches, "the Pastors and theologians of our Churches."[14]

Still another revolutionary feature of this encyclical, the invitation to join the search for a new way of exercising the primacy, is not confined only to Orthodox and Catholic bishops and theologians. The Pope addresses all Christian Churches and communions, issuing the same invitation: "Could not the real but imperfect communion existing between us persuade Church leaders and their theologians to engage with me in a patient and fraternal dialog on this subject . . . ?" (*UUS* §96).

All Christian leaders and theologians are invited to take part in the search for a new kind of papacy. Toward the end of the encyclical, Pope John Paul II again speaks of his own feeling and awareness:

> Whatever relates to the unity of all Christian communities clearly forms part of the concerns of the primacy. As Bishop of Rome I am fully aware . . . that Christ ardently desires the full and visible communion of all those Communities in which . . . his Spirit dwells. I am convinced that I have a particular responsibility in this regard. (*UUS* §95)

The invitation to a common effort to discover a new way of exercising the papacy comes not only from reasons of the mind but also from reasons of the heart. Lack of unity burdens the heart of the Pope and weighs on his conscience.

Taking the Initiative

Given the urgency of Christian unity, it can no longer be justified to wait for the other churches or ecclesial communions

---

[14] Some have said that the invitation to probe the papacy was directed only to non-Catholics. This passage of the encyclical, however, clearly dispels that idea.

to take the first step. The Catholic Church must be bold in showing firm—not timid—confidence in him who makes all things new.[15] Taking the initiative is specifically mentioned in the Vatican II Decree on Ecumenism, where Catholics are urged to make "the first approaches towards" those brothers and sisters who do not have full communion with us (§4).[16]

But taking the first step is not confined merely to gestures of friendship. This becomes clear in the very next sentence, where reform and action within the Catholic Church are called for: "But their special duty is to make a careful and honest appraisal of whatever needs to be renewed in the catholic household itself."[17] The Latin original of words here translated as "whatever needs to be renewed" reads, *"quae . . . renovanda et efficienda sunt."* This means "what *must* be renewed and what *must* be carried out," conveying the sense of duty and obligation.[18] It is not an option but a necessity.

In the interest of Christian unity, the Catholic household must examine its conscience. It must ask what things that give offense and create obstacles can be changed or even rejected. This would suggest that the effectiveness of fraternal dialogue with other Christians is dependent on and presupposes a parallel fraternal dialogue among Catholics themselves about internal reform in the Catholic Church with a goal of Christian unity.[19] The Pope rightly points out,

> John even goes so far as to state: "If we say that we have not sinned, we make him a liar, and his word is not in us." *Such*

---

[15] See Bernard Sesboüé, S.J., "Le ministère de communion du Pape," *Etudes* 384 (June 1996): 805–8.

[16] See *Decrees of the Ecumenical Councils,* ed. Tanner, 2:911.

[17] Ibid.

[18] See Charles E. Bennett, *New Latin Grammar* (Boston: Allyn & Bacon, 1946), §8, p. 220.

[19] In light of the call of this encyclical for dialogue within the Catholic Church, it is interesting to recall the spirited opposition against Cardinal Joseph Bernardin of Chicago when he proposed the same kind of dialogue among factions within the Catholic Church in the United States.

*a radical exhortation to acknowledge our condition as sin-
ners* ought also to mark the spirit which we bring to ecumenical dialog. (*UUS* §34)

The ecumenical dialogue, says the Pope, must become an
examination of conscience which admits the sins of the pastors but also acknowledges sinful structures "which have
contributed and can still contribute to division and to the
reinforcing of division" (*UUS* §34). The parallel fraternal
dialogue within the Catholic Church, then, must search for
internal reform both of the sinful actions of pastors, that is,
bishops and popes, and of sinful structures and sinful policies. This examination must work through the lens of unity:
How has all this impeded and how is it still impeding Christian unity?

Is the End of Division the End of Diversity?

Some non-Catholic Christians are hesitant about full communion with the Catholic Church because they fear that it
will mean the end of diversity.[20] This is not surprising, as
these Christians observe the struggles of Catholic bishops
seeking authentic inculturation in various parts of the world
and the constraints constantly being placed on them. A case
in point is the recent Synod on Asia, where some Asian bishops attributed the Church's lack of success in Asia to the fact
that it had to wear a Western face in its liturgy and theology.[21]

John Paul II forthrightly takes up this issue. He says, "In
accordance with the hope expressed by Pope Paul VI, our
declared purpose is to re-establish together full unity in legitimate diversity" (*UUS* §57). He goes on to show that diversity is not just something to be grudgingly tolerated. It is in

---

[20] See "Search for Unity Should Start Again, Cardinal Pleads," *The
Tablet,* June 20, 1998, p. 822.

[21] See "Will Rome Listen to the Asian Bishops?" *The Tablet,* May 2,
1998, p. 565.

fact a quality that greatly strengthens the life and mission of the Church. He bases this position on the teaching of Vatican II itself. "[L]egitimate diversity is in no way opposed to the Church's unity, but rather enhances her splendor and contributes greatly to the fulfillment of her mission" (*UUS* §50). To the degree that legitimate diversity is suppressed, the splendor of the Church is dimmed and its mission diminished. Uniformity not required by the integrity of faith or the exigencies of unity and communion is detrimental to the vitality of Church life and undermines the search for unity among Christians. Actions, then, such as those mentioned above, serve only to reveal the very wide gulf that exists between papal teaching and curial practice and how harmful this is to Christian unity.

The Vatican II Decree on Ecumenism teaches that rigid and pervasive uniformity is the enemy of true catholicity:

> While preserving unity in essentials, let all members of the Church, according to the office entrusted to each, preserve a proper freedom in the various forms of spiritual life and discipline, in the variety of liturgical rites, even in the theological elaborations of revealed truth. In all things let charity be exercised. If the faithful are true to this course of action, they will be giving even richer expression to the authentic catholicity of the Church, and, at the same time, to her apostolicity.[22]

Johannes Feiner, in his commentary on this passage, says:

> If the faithful give "richer expression" to the catholicity of the Church in this way, so, at the same time, the apostolicity of the Church will also be more fully realized, as the text points out. The basic principle of the "Apostolic Council," "to lay upon you no greater burden than these necessary things" (Acts 15:28), the recognition of diverse charismata, the readiness of the Apostle Paul to become a Jew to the Jews and one outside the law to those outside the law (I Cor. 9:20f), are characteristic of the attitude of the apostolic

---

[22] *Decrees of the Ecumenical Councils*, ed Tanner, 2:912.

church. Uniformity and centralism are certainly ill fitted to demonstrate the identity of the present day Church with the apostolic Church.[23]

It is Feiner's opinion that uniformist and centralizing policies have positively damaged the true catholicity of the Church.[24]

While the Pope does not spell out in detail what legitimate diversity is, he strongly endorses the principle of diversity and embraces diversity as a necessary quality of Christian unity: "[O]ur declared purpose is to re-establish together full unity in legitimate diversity" (*UUS* §57).

Along with communion, diversity was a quality of the early Church. The New Testament itself and the history of the first two hundred years manifest considerable differences both in structure and practice among the communities that formed the one Church. Raymond Brown has shown how even among the churches Paul founded, some had bishops but others did not.[25] In the early second century, Antioch had a single bishop, while the Church at Rome probably did not have a single bishop until later.[26] Churches in Asia celebrated Easter according to the Jewish calendar on the fourteenth day of Nisan, the Passover, no matter what day of the week it was. Rome celebrated Easter on a Sunday.[27] The objection may be raised to this diversity that Pope Victor, around the year 195, strenuously objected to the Eastern practice and even excommunicated the province of Asia for its refusal to celebrate Easter on Sunday. While this is true, there are several instructive factors touching the Easter controversy which must be mentioned. First, it seems that when

[23] Johannes Feiner, in *Commentary on the Documents of Vatican II*, ed. Herbert Vorgrimler (New York: Herder & Herder, 1968), 2:91.

[24] Ibid., 90.

[25] Raymond E. Brown, S.S., *Priest and Bishop* (New York: Paulist Press, 1970), 82ff.

[26] Ibid., 53–54. See also Klaus Schatz, *Papal Primacy* (Collegeville, Minn.: Liturgical Press, 1996), 4.

[27] Schatz, *Papal Primacy,* 11–12.

things settled down after the conflict the two practices did in fact continue side by side up to the fifth century. But in addition, a significant ecclesiological factor is that many of the bishops of the time regarded Pope Victor's act of excommunication as extreme and spoke up urging him to back down. Included among these bishops was Irenaeus.[28] On the one hand, then, this incident shows that before the end of the second century Rome had a sense of responsibility and a consciousness of authority in the whole Church, even the East. On the other hand, it also shows that bishops of the Church had a consciousness of an obligation to speak forthrightly when they believed the *way* Roman authority was being exercised was excessive. There is no indication in Irenaeus or elsewhere that Victor's authority to intervene was questioned. Such diversity in the ancient Church raises the possibility that within the communion of a reunited Church today there could be room for diversity in structures and practices. As in the ancient Church, there could also be diversity in how the one faith is expressed and which aspects of faith are emphasized.

The Doctrinal Core of Papal Primacy

What is essential to primacy? What does *Ut unum sint* see as its irreducible doctrinal core? First and above all the Pope mentions vigilance over the whole Church and the service of unity and communion:

> The mission of the Bishop of Rome within the College of all the Pastors consists precisely in "keeping watch" (*episkopein*). . . . With the power and authority without which such an office would be illusory, the Bishop of Rome must ensure the communion of all the Churches. For this reason, he is the first servant of unity. (*UUS* §94)

---

[28] Irenaeus was bishop of Lyons in the late second century. He is sometimes called the father of theology. He died around the year 202.

Some non-Catholic Christians have expressed a favorable attitude toward a papacy that would be a primacy of honor, a ceremonial precedence without real authority. This expression derives from canons of the fourth-century Council of Constantinople and the fifth-century Council of Chalcedon, where it was applied to the bishop of Rome.[29] However, in a careful study of the use of the expression "primacy of honor" in ancient times, Brian Daley has shown that it did not mean a merely ceremonial leadership. It included, as Pope John Paul stated above, "the power and authority without which such an office would be illusory" and was understood in this sense in both ancient councils.[30]

The Pope then states that the primacy is exercised at four different levels (*UUS* §94). The primacy exists within the College of Bishops. It consists in "keeping watch." It has true authority. It must ensure communion.

All of this suggests that there is a certain latitude for modification and adaptation in the way the papal office is exercised as the good of unity may require. The papal office does not have to be exercised in the twenty-first century the way it was in 1945 or 1073. That the Pope has in mind greater flexibility is indicated by the fact that he holds up in *Ut unum sint* the crucial apostolic principle of imposing nothing beyond what is necessary. "In this process, one must not impose any burden beyond that which is strictly necessary" (*UUS* §78).

The Pope points out seven specific instances of primatial vigilance and service of unity (*UUS* §94). They are:

---

[29] For an Orthodix analysis of these canons, see Archbishop Peter L'Huillier, *The Church of the Ancient Councils* (Crestwood, N.Y.: St. Vladimir's Seminary Press, 1996). Archbishop Peter states that the fathers at Chalcedon had no intention of putting in doubt the primacy of Old Rome. "The authorized commentary of the decree given by the imperial commissioners and the letter of the council to Pope Leo were absolutely clear on this point" (p. 272).

[30] See Brian E. Daley, "Position and Patronage in the Early Church: The Original Meaning of 'Primacy of Honour,'" *Journal of Theological Studies* n.s. 44, no. 2 (October 1993): 529–33.

- Vigilance over the handing down of the word
- Vigilance over the celebration of the liturgy and the sacraments
- Vigilance over the Church's mission, discipline and the Christian life
- Vigilance over the requirements of the common good of the Church should anyone be tempted to overlook it in the pursuit of personal interests
- The primatial duty to admonish, to caution, and to declare at times that this or that opinion . . . is irreconcilable with the unity of faith
- The primatial duty to speak in the name of all the Pastors in communion with him when circumstances require it
- The primatial authority—under very specific (and limited) conditions to declare *ex cathedra* that a certain doctrine belongs to the deposit of faith

Having listed these components of the primatial office, the Pope makes a statement that would probably surprise many Catholics:

> *All this* however *must always* [emphasis added] be done in communion. When the Catholic Church affirms that the office of the Bishop of Rome corresponds to the will of Christ, she does not separate this office from the mission entrusted to the whole body of Bishops, who are also "vicars and ambassadors of Christ." The Bishop of Rome is a member of the "College," and the Bishops are his brothers in the ministry. (*UUS* §95)

The force of this declaration would seem to be that the normal mode of the exercise of papal authority will be collaborative and consultative, one that respects legitimate church structures such as the patriarchates and episcopal conferences, and one that is dedicated to preserving diversity within the framework of unity.

A Model for the Papacy: The First Millennium

Pope John Paul holds up the first millennium as one example to guide the search for a new way of exercising the primacy: "For a whole millennium Christians were united in a
'brotherly fraternal communion of faith and sacramental
life. . . . If disagreements in belief and discipline arose among
them, the Roman See acted by common consent as moderator' (*UUS* §95)."

It is worth noting that this text, which incorporates a text
of Vatican II, describes the Roman See as "moderator."
"Moderator" is a Latin word and is used in the Latin text of
the council. It includes the meaning of "guide" or "someone
who sets the limits."[31] The word does not of itself imply centralized government or constant involvement in the life of
the individual churches.[32] This is evident from two things.
First, the contingent way in which intervention of the Pope
is described: "*if* [emphasis added] disagreements . . . arose."
And, second, from the mention of the patriarchal churches
in this section of the Decree on Ecumenism. A portion of the
council text, not explicitly cited in the encyclical, says, "For
many centuries the churches of the east and the west followed their separate ways though linked in a union of faith
and sacramental life."[33] The patriarchates contributed to the
genuine diversity of the Church and constituted "a balancing
force against an excessive centralization within the universal
Church."[34]

It is also significant that in listing the functions of the primacy and in speaking of the first millennium the Pope does
not use the language of "primacy of jurisdiction." This is not

---

[31] See Charlton T. Lewis and Charles Short, *A Latin Dictionary* (New
York: Oxford University Press, 1962), s.v. *moderator,* p. 1154.

[32] "Decree on Ecumenism," in *Commentary on the Documents of Vatican II,* ed. Vorgrimler, 2:129ff., article 14.

[33] *Decrees of the Ecumenical Councils,* ed. Tanner, 2:916.

[34] Feiner, in *Commentary on the Documents of Vatican II,* ed. Vorgrimler, 2:130.

to say that he is questioning or denying it, but he does not project back into the first millennium a concept and language that did not exist then. The practice of the primacy as understood in the second millennium did not exist in the first. Commenting in 1983 on the final report of the Anglican-Roman Catholic International Commission I, Cardinal Joseph Ratzinger wrote, "The early Church did indeed know nothing of Roman primacy in practice, in the sense of Roman Catholic theology of the second millennium. . . ."[35] This is a qualified statement. It is not saying that the early Church knew nothing of the Roman primacy, but only that the Roman primacy was not practiced in the way it is in the second millennium.

In *Ut unum sint* the Pope does not confine himself to generalities. He also mentions ecclesiastical structures and practices of the first millennium:

> In its historical survey the Council Decree *Unitatis Redintegratio*[36] has in mind the unity, which in spite of everything, was experienced in the first millennium and in a certain sense now serves as a model. . . . The *structures* [emphasis added] of the Church in the East and in the West evolved in reference to that Apostolic heritage. Her unity during the first millennium was maintained within those same structures through the Bishops, Successors of the Apostles, in communion with the Bishop of Rome. If today at the end of the second millennium we are seeking to restore full communion, it is to that unity, *thus structured* [emphasis added], which we must look. . . .
>
> The *structures* [emphasis added] of unity which existed before the separation are a heritage of experience that guides our common path towards re-establishment of full communion. (*UUS* §§55, 56)

---

[35] See Charles M. Murphy, "Collegiality: An Essay Toward Better Understanding," *Theological Studies* 46 (1985): 45–46. The Ratzinger citation is found in "Anglican-Catholic Dialogue: Its Problems and Hopes," *Insight* 1, no. 3 (March 1983): 5.

[36] The Latin title means "The Restoration of Unity" and is the title of the Vatican II Document on Christian Unity.

For Pope John Paul II, the first millennium is critical. It is a model and a guide particularly in its structures. To look back to the first millennium as a model is to place structures of collegiality before us and point to collegial modes of exercising the primatial and episcopal office in the Church. These were characteristic of the Church of the first millennium.

In his excellent history of the primacy, Klaus Schatz has shown how the exercise and understanding of the Roman primacy underwent a development during the whole of the first millennium. It was not only synodal and collegial action at the regional level that maintained universal communion, but communion of all the patriarchs with one another and in a special way with the bishop of Rome, which in the first millennium marked the Church as one.[37] And gradually during the first millennium Rome emerged as the center of communion of all the Churches.[38]

But Schatz points out that "[u]nity in the first millennium is an equivocal concept. It looked very different in different eras and was very differently interpreted, not only in the West and East, but especially within the Eastern Church itself."[39] In the first millennium the idea did not exist that the bishop of Rome would intervene in the affairs of the other Churches on a routine basis or in normal times. On the other hand, there is a continuing and consistent witness that Rome is an indispensable norm of ecclesial communion and that the bishop of Rome has a unique role of primacy in the communion of all the Churches. In periods of crisis, especially those having to do with matters of faith, there was a conviction even among eastern authorities, that these could be definitively resolved only in union with Rome and not apart from it.[40]

---

[37] See Schatz, *Papal Primacy*, 17–38.

[38] Ibid., 17–28.

[39] Ibid., 59. See also Yves Congar, *Eglise et Papauté* (Paris: Editions du Cerf, 1994), 272–73.

[40] See Schatz, *Papal Primacy*, 59–60.

If, then, the first millennium is used as a basis for dialogue about finding "a way of exercising the primacy which . . . is . . . open to a new situation" (*UUS* §95), it would include a recognition of a unique role for the bishop of Rome in dealing with crises, especially crises of faith. It would not include a routine role for the bishop of Rome in the affairs of the Eastern Churches.

The First Millennium and Other Christians

Respect for the autonomy[41] of the patriarchs and Eastern Churches within the framework of communion, would also have implications for other Christian Churches, notably the Anglican and Protestant Churches:

> It should finally be noted that the statements of the decree [i.e., the Decree on Ecumenism of Vatican II] concerning the (relative) autonomy of the Eastern Churches are also significant as a testimony to the other separated Churches, and therefore have a general ecumenical importance; a union of separated Churches can only be thought of as a union of different "types of Church" which, within the unity sought by Christ, would preserve their own distinctive nature and their "canonical" autonomy.[42]

Pope John Paul II presents his vision of the minimal requirements of the papal office required to serve unity and

---

[41] Here the autonomy of the patriarchs is mentioned. It is applied also to other Christian Churches or communions that might enter full communion with Rome. The use of this word creates a certain uneasiness especially for those who have a strictly monarchical, sovereign idea of the papacy. However, the word autonomy has to be understood as autonomy within communion and thus distinct from independence. Autonomy, in fact, is used of religious orders and congregations in the Church. Thus canon 586 of the Code of Canon Law (1983) states: "For individual institutes there is acknowledged a rightful autonomy of life, especially of governance, by which they enjoy their own discipline in the Church and have the power to preserve their own patrimony intact as mentioned in can. 578."

[42] Feiner, in *Commentary on the Documents of Vatican II,* ed. Vorgrimler, 2:138.

at the same time to preserve diversity. The first point he makes is that there is a distinction between what is essential to the papal office and the way it is exercised.

> I have a particular responsibility . . . in heeding the request made of me to find a *way of exercising* [emphasis added] the primacy which, while in no way renouncing what is essential to its mission, is nonetheless open to a new situation. (*UUS* §95)

This means that, preserving the basic core of the papal office, it can be exercised in different ways in different times and circumstances. The papacy can change—and has changed greatly in its two-thousand year history.

The encyclical *Ut unum sint* is without question a revolutionary document. No other Pope has said to Catholics and all other Christians what I might paraphrase in this way:

> I realize that the papal primacy is a serious obstacle to our union. Let's talk about it and see what can be done. There are certain basic elements that the papal primacy will always have to have. But beyond that things can change. There can be a new way of papal primacy. I cannot say what that would be. I need your help in trying to discover it.

The encyclical *Ut unum sint* is clearly precedent breaking and, in many respects, revolutionary. It calls for a discussion of the papacy by all Christians with the goal of finding a new way of making it more a service of love than of domination. It holds up the synodal model of the Church in the first millennium and emphasizes that the pope is a member of the College of Bishops and that the primacy should be exercised in a collegial manner. It witnesses the fact that to embrace Vatican I and its teaching on the primacy of jurisdiction does not exclude a broader understanding of that primacy. It indicates that Vatican I was not the last word.[43]

The test of the credibility of *Ut unum sint* is how the primacy is exercised within the Catholic Church itself and

---

[43] Pottmeyer, *Towards a Papacy,* chapters 1–4.

whether the Catholic Church stands before the Christian world as a model of what is proposed in the encyclical. There is no realistic hope for Christian unity unless the Catholic Church is willing to take a serious look at itself as the Pope has asked. With this in mind, in succeeding chapters I will discuss the issue of criticism and public opinion within the Church, the collegiality of the episcopate, the system governing the appointment of bishops, the place of the College of Cardinals within the episcopate and the role of the Roman Curia. Each of these issues has an important place in the search for Christian unity. Each of them has a bearing on the reform and the exercise of the primacy.

Chapter 2

Reform and Criticism
in the Church

Pope John Paul II has called for a dialogue to "find a way of exercising the primacy . . . open to a new situation" (*UUS* §95). This means that the present mode of exercise of the primacy is not entirely adequate in responding to the new situation. One factor in finding this "new way of exercising the primacy" will be criticism of the present, and identification of some specific factors connected with the exercise of the primacy which create obstacles to Christian unity. But before responding directly to the papal invitation, it is important to set the framework for a response by taking a look at the place of reform and criticism in the life of the Church.

Reform in the Church

One reason for resistance to reform is that deeply embedded in the memory of the Church are the Protestant Reformers of the sixteenth century, who used the word "reform" to include rejection of the papacy, rejection of the priesthood, the Mass, the intercession of Our Lady and the saints, monastic and religious life, and other things. Such an idea of reform is repugnant to Catholic sensibilities and incompatible with Catholic faith. An example of this kind of anti-reform thinking that exists even today is Pope Gregory XVI, who in the nineteenth century declared that the Church cannot possibly be reformed "as if she could be considered subject to defect or obscuration or other misfortune."[1]

---

[1] Pope Gregory XVI, Encyclical Letter *Mirari Vos*, August 15, 1832;

Yet paradoxically, notwithstanding Gregory XVI, the solemn Magisterium of the Church has continually used the word "reform." The Council of Trent enacted at least ninety-six canons or specific directives explicitly entitled "reform."[2] In fact, after defining the content of Catholic faith against the Reformers' attacks, the first priority of Trent was Church reform.[3]

The Second Vatican Council also spoke of the reform of the Church. Thus the Decree on Ecumenism states: "In its pilgrimage on earth Christ summons the church to continual reformation, of which it is always in need, in so far as it is an institution of human beings here on earth" (§6).[4] From these words, it might be thought that the council is talking only about the personal conversion of individual Christians. But this is not the case. The decree continues,

> Thus if, in various times and circumstances, there have been deficiencies in moral conduct or in church discipline, or even in the way that church teaching has been formulated—to be carefully distinguished from the deposit of faith itself—these should be set right in the proper way at the opportune moment. (§6)

Church practice, law, and even Church teaching—all are subject to reform and "should be set right in the proper way at the opportune moment.[5]

Claudia Carlen, I.H.M., *The Papal Encyclicals 1740–1878* (N.P.: McGrath Publishing, 1981), 237, §10.

[2] See *Decrees of the Ecumenical Councils,* ed. Norman P. Tanner, S.J., (New York: Sheed & Ward; Washington, D.C.: Georgetown University Press, 1990), 2:660–797 (Council of Trent).

[3] Hubert Jedin, *Crisis and Closure of the Council of Trent,* Sheed & Ward Stagbooks (London/Melbourne: Sheed & Ward, 1967), 121.

[4] Decree on Ecumenism (*Unitatis Redintegratio*), cited throughout this book according to *Decrees of the Ecumenical Councils,* ed. Tanner, 2:908–20.

[5] The council text speaks only of the *formulation* of Church teaching. If all that can be changed is the formulation, then, of course, divinely revealed truth or dogmas taught by the Church are understood. But this

For Vatican II, continual reform is not only necessary for the individual and for the Church as such, but it is crucial for any hope of Christian unity. The English text of the council document reads, "Such renewal (reform) therefore has notable ecumenical importance" (§6). This seems like a bland platitude, but the Latin text of the decree uses the word *insigne,* here translated as "notable." *Insigne,* however, does not simply mean "notable." It means the distinctive mark of something. Reform, then, according to the council, is the hallmark, the "insignia" of the Catholic Church's ecumenical hopes and action.[6] The Catholic Church cannot hope for Christian unity unless she herself undertakes her own internal reform.

Vatican II not only calls for reform; it mentions with approval a number of reform movements in the twentieth century which prepared for the council: the biblical movement, the liturgical movement, the lay movements, which though not mentioned by name would include such movements as the Young Christian Worker movement in Belgium and France, and Catholic Action. Most of these movements were characterized by a return to the sources, to the Bible, to the patristic heritage, and by an effort to appraise the present situation of the Church, especially the pastoral situation, in light of these sources.[7] But the movements were not confined

---

still leaves room for teachings of the Church that are not irreformable and can be changed not merely in their formulation but in their substance as well and may in time even be rejected. For example, the official Catholic position before Vatican II was that the ideal was that the Catholic Church would be the official Church in a nation, that other arrangements could be tolerated. Vatican II rejected this teaching and held that the only thing the Church asked in society was freedom to fulfill her mission, not any special status. There are other examples in the course of history.

[6] See Charlton T. Lewis and Charles Short, *A Latin Dictionary* (New York: Oxford University Press, 1962), s.v. *insigne,* p. 965.

[7] This is a difference between the reform movements before Vatican II and the more or less anti-reform movements of today. The reform movements that preceded Vatican II derived their inspiration from a deeper

to theory or to exclusively intellectual circles. Practical experiments were also under way in the years before the council.

Two such experiments in the years before the council come to mind: the worker priests in France and Belgium[8] and the quiet experimentation with the vernacular language in the Mass in parts of France and Germany.

Large numbers of people were alienated from the Church in Europe over a century and a half, so much so that a French best-seller in the early fifties bore the title "France Pagan?" The Church had lost the working classes in France and Belgium. Pope Pius XI himself confirmed this when he said in 1927 to the well-known Belgian priest Abbe Cardijn, that the great scandal of the Church in the nineteenth century was that she had lost the working classes.

In an effort to respond to the dechristianization of the workers, these priests, about one hundred in number, got jobs in factories, where they could be close to their people and share their hardships and insecurities. The worker priests lasted just about ten years; then, because of questions about the priest's proper role and his relationship to the secular order, as well as for various other reasons, this experiment was discontinued. Nevertheless, it was an honest effort to bring the workers back to the Church, to reform the relationship of the Church to the world, and to develop the theological and pastoral meaning of the priesthood.

Another experiment to win people back to the Church lay in efforts in Germany and France in the years preceding Vatican II to introduce the vernacular into the celebration of the

---

study of the Bible, the fathers, and Church history. They were also inspired by an analysis of the existing pastoral situation of the Church in light of these sources. The contemporary anti-reform movements do not emphasize the sources—scripture, the fathers, etc. They emphasize "tradition" and call themselves "traditionalists," but it is in the narrow sense of what has happened in the last 150 years or, at most, the last 400 years.

[8] See D. Robert, "Worker Priests," in *New Catholic Encyclopedia* (New York: McGraw-Hill, 1967), 14:1019–20.

liturgy in place of the beautiful but incomprehensible Latin enjoined by Church law.[9] Priests seemed pastorally distant from the people, and the liturgy was inaccessible to them except as passive spectators. Many lost interest.[10] As a student in Rome in the early fifties I had the opportunity to experience both the soaring beauty of the Latin liturgy and the genuine pastoral efforts to bring people back through the vernacular. Unforgettable to me are my visits to the Abbey of Maria Laach in Germany, to the Abbey of Solesmes in France, and, more often, my visits to the Abbey of San Anselmo in Rome. Most people would never experience the contemplative beauty of the liturgy as celebrated in these monasteries. But alongside that experience was my opportunity to visit ordinary parishes in France and Germany and to hear German and French used here and there in the liturgical dialogue with the people or in other parts of the Mass. It was refreshing and pointed to what was to come. Remembering now that the movement toward the vernacular in the years preceding Vatican II had among other aims to remedy the alienation of large numbers from the Church, it is ironic that today, after the council, there are those who are promoting the return to Latin.

Both the reform movements and these pastoral experiments show how it was a partnership of both scholarship and pastoral experience that shaped the reforming Vatican

---

[9] It is well known that the Council of Trent considered introducing the vernacular. The first American bishop, John Carroll, also petitioned Rome for introduction of the vernacular in the United States. His reasons: the United States, as he said, was a Protestant country and Catholics a small minority. Use of Latin would only reinforce prejudice against the Catholic Church as "foreign." Second, he believed that use of Latin would also be an obstacle to conversions in the United States. His petition was denied.

[10] In a discussion of alienation and as a reason for not taking it seriously, one always encounters appeals to the fact that there are those who remain faithful through everything. This is true. There are the devout who endure all things in faith and find God in all things. But they are not the great masses of people for whom Christ died and whose needs the Church is also sent to meet.

Council II. There was a consciousness at all levels that reform was necessary.

Besides the reform movements, the two World Wars, with their unspeakable horror, also gave a new incentive for reform. Catholics, sharing both peril and hope in the crucible of war side by side with non-Catholics, came to see that there had to be a way of breaking down the barriers existing until then. The formalisms and rigidities of some aspects of Church life no longer seemed to fit the new kind of world people were beginning to experience or the new insights into the New Testament and Christian history that pastoral experience and scholarship were bringing with them. There was an atmosphere of change, of taking stock, of imagining new ways, an atmosphere of expectation. A psychology of reform was definitely taking shape.

Personal Experience Shapes John XXIII

Like a great rock continually bathed by the force of the surrounding ocean, a then unknown figure was both experiencing and weighing these currents in the Church and in society, and a vision gradually formed in him which was to have a profound and lasting effect on the Catholic Church. He had quite a diversified experience of life that brought him into contact with a number of different kinds of people and situations. As a seminarian, the future Pope John XXIII interrupted his theological studies in the fall of 1901 for one year to serve as a soldier in the Italian army. After his ordination, he was recalled to military service in World War I, first as a sergeant in the medical corps and then as a lieutenant in the chaplain corps.[11] He was later apostolic delegate in Bulgaria, Turkey, and Greece. After nearly twenty years in Eastern Europe, he was sent to France as papal nuncio in 1944.

---

[11] The story is told that after he became Pope, he received a group of Italian military and introduced himself as Sergeant Roncalli. For more complete information on John XXIII's background, see R. Trisco, "John XXIII, Pope," in *New Catholic Encyclopedia*, 7:1015–20.

There he observed firsthand the pastoral and scholarly movements so alive there. Years of personal, brotherly relationships with Orthodox and Protestant Christians in Eastern Europe and France, the experience of war, his varied contacts, and his personal reflection and reading all deepened his conviction of the need for reform and renewal if the Church was to fulfill its mission in a changed and continually changing world. There is evidence to indicate that during his years in France he read Yves Congar's work *True and False Reform in the Church*.[12] A work of such depth, lucidity, and scholarship must have made a strong impression on him.

It is not surprising, then, that in the first hundred days after his election as Pope, John XXIII convoked the Second Vatican Council under the theme of *"aggiornamento."*[13] The Church had to open the windows. She could not make the mistake of the nineteenth century by closing herself against the movement of history and scholarship, by failing to read the signs of the times.[14] John, a lover of history, no doubt saw what a tragedy it would be if the Church, intransigent

---

[12] See Yves Congar, *Vraie et Fausse Réforme dans l'Eglise* (2nd ed.; Paris: Editions du Cerf, 1969), preface, p. 8 n. 2.

[13] Literally, *aggiornamento* means "bringing up to date." It meant bringing the Church up to date, reforming the Church in terms of the needs of the times, so that the Church could be more effective in the fulfillment of her mission and not become, as John was to say, "an archaeological museum."

[14] When such observations are made, there are always those who object that the Church cannot be a sponge blindly absorbing what goes on in the world around it. This should be obvious. But to those who know history, it should also be obvious that when the Church is closed and *only* negative about the currents of change and history rather than engaging them and "testing the spirit, clinging to the good and rejecting of evil" she runs the risk of disaster. These currents and movements usually have both a good and a bad side. Discernment requires examining and admitting both. For a study of this problem as it occurred in the sixteenth century, see, e.g., Barbara Tuchman, *The March of Folly* (New York: Ballentine, 1985), chapter 3.

and fearful, were to risk in the twentieth century the losses she suffered in the sixteenth and the nineteenth centuries because of a refusal to act until it was too little too late. It is ironic and illustrative of this penchant to delay too long, that after several centuries of calls for reform from within the Church, the Council of Trent did not hold its first working session until twenty-eight years after Luther addressed his ninety-five theses to the archbishop of Mainz, and just a little more than five weeks before Luther's death.[15] The incurable wound had by then been inflicted. Unity—for centuries to come—became impossible.[16] Church authorities did not take the danger seriously enough and waited too long.[17] By the time of Luther's death, it was too late.[18]

John XXIII rightly emphasized that history is the teacher of life.[19] History thus shows that far from being an idea foreign or inimical to the Church, reform has been a constant and recurring theme, from the eleventh-century Popes Leo

---

[15] Luther's theses were devised on the occasion of the selling of indulgences to support the building of St. Peter's Basilica in Rome. The story of Luther posting the theses on the door of Wittenberg's castle church first appears after Luther's death and is not regarded as historically verified. See *The Oxford Encyclopedia of the Reformation* (New York: Oxford University Press, 1996), s.v. "Luther," 2:462. Also Jedin states that as late as 1562 the work of reforming the Church had not even begun. See Jedin, *Crisis and Closure*, 44.

[16] See *Oxford Encyclopedia of the Reformation*, 2:461–67.

[17] In more recent times, the social encyclicals of the Popes, beginning with Leo XIII (1878–1903), and the encyclicals on the liturgy were not really taken seriously in large sectors of the Church until Vatican II. Neither of these types of encyclical figured prominently in mainstream seminary education during the first part of the twentieth century.

[18] See Klaus Schatz, *Papal Primacy* (Collegeville, Minn.: Liturgical Press, 1996), 177. Speaking of the crucial and positive role played by the papacy in moments of crisis in the Church, he notes the great exception to the rule, "the great Western schism, brought about by the papacy itself, which the papacy was then unable to resolve."

[19] John XXIII, "Opening Speech to the Council," in *The Documents of Vatican II*, ed. Walter M. Abbott, S.J. (New York: America Press, 1966), 712.

IX and Gregory VII[20] through John Paul II. The failures of
the Church in the second millennium—the loss of whole
peoples to Catholic unity in the sixteenth century, the loss of
the workers in the nineteenth, the alienation of the intellec-
tuals in the twentieth—have been due not so much to reform
within the Church as to the *lack* of timely reform, the failure
to weigh carefully enough the signs of the times, and the failure to act in time.

Criticism—the Matrix of Reform

That the dynamic of continual reform in the Church has not
ceased is attested by Pope John Paul's encyclical *Ut unum
sint* (§95). And if the Church is in need of continual reform,
she is necessarily in need of continual criticism. Reform and
criticism go together.

But if there is resistance to reform within the Church,
there is even more resistance to criticism. The Italian journalist Giancarlo Zizola reports Cardinal Angelo Sodano,
Vatican Secretary of State, as saying, "If you love, you do
not criticize."[21] This saying well captures the attitude of
many in Rome and of many Catholics all around the world.
Why is this? Has it always been so?

Criticism before the Council of Trent

History, the teacher of life, indicates that this abhorrence of
criticism has not always been the prevailing attitude.
Throughout the fifteenth and sixteenth centuries prior to the
Council of Trent, vigorous criticism was frequently linked
with reform by the preachers at the papal court, even when
preaching in the presence of the Pope. "Insofar as these criticisms were directed against churchmen, they fit the pattern

---

[20] See *Oxford Encyclopedia of the Reformation*, s.v. "Reform," 3:392.
[21] Giancarlo Zizola, *Il Successore* (Rome/Bari: Laterza, 1997), 122:
"Chi ama non critica."

of an age when criticisms of the Church and the call for its reform were swelling and becoming increasingly strident."[22] Open criticism of the Pope and Church authorities was taken in stride. But it did not begin in the fifteenth century.

Early in the pontificate of Gregory VII in the eleventh century, his reforms were criticized by the German bishops at the Synod of Worms in 1076. They accused the Pope of violating apostolic structures and of taking the power of binding and loosing from the bishops.[23]

Art in this period was also critical, as the facades of many cathedrals witness.[24] Like these facades, the paintings of the saintly Fra Angelico depict monks, bishops, and popes condemned to hell. Literature follows the same line. For example, Dante in *The Divine Comedy* condemns even his contemporaries, Nicholas III, Boniface VIII, and Clement V, to eternal punishment.[25]

Criticism was also a common trait of saints and scholars of this period.[26] In a sermon, St. Bernard says:

> Yesterday we were saying that we should like to have leaders who actually guide us along our path, rather than the sort we have now. Our current "leaders" are just the opposite. . . . They love their perquisites, and they love them more than they love Christ. For they have given themselves over to Mammon. . . . Show me a bishop not more concerned with discharging his people's purses of their money than their souls of their sins. . . . Of course it is a waste of time to go on

---

[22] John W. O'Malley, S.J., *Praise and Blame in Renaissance Rome* (Durham, N.C.: Duke University Press, 1979), 241.

[23] See Yves Congar, *L'Eglise de Saint Augustin à l'époque moderne* (Paris: Editions du Cerf, 1996), 113.

[24] An example is the celebrated facade of the Church of St. Trophime in Arles.

[25] Dante Alighieri, *The Divine Comedy, Inferno,* canto 19 (see also canto 3).

[26] For a more thorough treatment of criticism, see José I. González Faus, S.J., *Where the Spirit Breathes* (Maryknoll, N.Y.: Orbis Books, 1989).

like this. They will pay no attention. . . . (*Homily 77 on the Song of Songs; PL* 183:1155–56)

St. Catherine of Siena, speaking of bishops, says: "Not only do they not give what they are in duty bound to give to the poor, but they rob them through simony and their hankering after money, selling the grace of the Holy Spirit."[27]

The twelfth-century abbot of Reichersberg, Gerhoh, one of the most distinguished theologians of the time, wrote a treatise on the corruption of the Church. He says:

> We write this treatise for the eyes of the Pope, that the Roman Curia—which according to the testimony of Peter [1 Pet. 5:13], is the church in Babylon (Babylon being a metaphor for Rome)—may use caution, strive to shake off its Babylonian shame, and present itself without wrinkle or blemish, both itself and the whole church which it ought to govern. For what we today call the Roman Curia or Court, and used to call the Roman Church, is anything but without blemish. (*Commentarium in Psalmos* 64; *PL* 194:9)

Even the fourteenth-century camerlengo Pedro de Aliaco writes:

> How often we beg God in the Church that he would teach us to condemn the things of earth and love the things of heaven. . . . Then how comes it that Christ is so condemned in the Roman Curia, and gold is preferred? Why is the good of unity in the universal church forgotten, although it is the good that all should seek—all the more intensely, the more exalted the dignity of the seeker?[28]

These examples show that criticism in this period was robust and forthright. Yet it was done within the framework of love for the Church and respect for the papal and priestly office. This kind of criticism was not a summons to reject the Church or her teaching or her sacramental life. Critics in this

---

[27] *Catherine of Siena: The Dialog* (New York: Paulist Press, 1980), 232.

[28] González Faus, *Where the Spirit Breathes*, 31.

period understood the difference between identifying abuses and calling into question substantive elements of the Church's faith and apostolic structure. Figures such as St. Bernard and St. Catherine are also witnesses that love for the Church does not in fact preclude criticism.

The Reformation and the Negative Attitude to Criticism

Things changed with the Reformation. Because of the strident rejection by the Reformers of substantive elements of Church life and teaching, discomfort with use of the word "reform" and grim resistance to criticism developed within the Catholic Church. Prior to the sixteenth-century Council of Trent, criticism, even though forceful and public, had a sort of "in the family" quality to it. But beginning with the Reformation and the fierce divisions it brought with it, the Catholic Church saw criticism as a weapon that would be used by her enemies against the Church.

In the early decades of the sixteenth century, as the Reformers were making greater and greater strides and becoming more and more critical, an event took place that had a decisive influence on the attitude toward criticism in the Church. In November of 1536 Pope Paul III, with a council in mind, created a commission to make recommendations about the pressing issues facing the Church.[29] The head of this commission was Cardinal Gasparo Contarini, a learned, distinguished, and holy man. The commission also included the future Paul IV and the Englishman Cardinal Reginald Pole. It is significant that Paul III, like John Paul II in a later age, took the initiative to ask for criticism of the existing situation. The report was presented on March 9, 1537, after approximately four months in preparation.

The Contarini report stated clearly that

---

[29] See John C. Olin, *Catholic Reform* (New York: Fordham University Press, 1990), 65–79.

all abuses were the result of exaggerated claims made by curial jurists about the absolute nature of papal power, and sin-
gled out for special blame their teaching that the pope was
free to do as he pleased with the material and spiritual goods
of the church. . . . Rome was held responsible for the lack of
discipline and order and for abuses throughout the church.[30]

In considerable detail the report went on to bring out the
abuses of simony, the widespread failure of bishops to live in
or care for their dioceses, the promotion of superstitious
devotions among the people, the ready ordination of men
who were unqualified and unprepared, and other abuses too
numerous to mention here.[31]

The report was leaked to a Roman printer, and a German
translation appeared in 1538 which brought caustic comments from Luther and only served to confirm his attacks on
the Catholic Church. This led Rome to fear that any kind of
criticism within the Church would play into the hands of the
Church's enemies, give grounds for their attacks, confuse the
people, and risk injury to their faith. From this developed the
conviction that criticism should be expressed only in the
most limited circles and that one must defend everything.
This resistance to all criticism led to an inflated idea of the
holiness and perfection of the Church so that any form of
criticism came to be viewed as an act of disloyalty, a breach-
ing of the ramparts. Gone are the days of St. Bernard and
Catherine of Siena.

Reverence for the Pope: A Reason against Criticism

Fear of inciting attacks on the Church thus became a prominent motive for opposing criticism from within the Church.
Reverence for the Pope, especially as it has developed since

---

[30] Elizabeth Johnson, "Consilium de Emendanda Ecclesia," in *Oxford Encyclopedia of the Reformation,* 1:415.
[31] See Olin, *Catholic Reform,* 65–79.

the nineteenth century, has been another factor militating against criticism from within the Church. In the nineteenth century, with its great social and cultural upheavals in Europe and the embattled state of the Pope resulting from attacks on and eventual seizure of the Papal States, the Pope came to be viewed as the one source of stability and truth and even to be identified with Christ. A Swiss bishop in a sermon at the beginning of Vatican I spoke of the "Incarnation of the Son of God in the old man in the Vatican."[32] Until this time the traditional motive for pilgrimage to Rome was to pray at the tombs of the apostles Peter and Paul. But now the motive for going to Rome was to see the Pope, and there began to develop the high priority of "devotion to the Pope."[33]

Also contributing to this development was the definition of the infallibility of the Pope in Vatican Council I. To understand this we must distinguish between what Vatican I actually taught and the popular consciousness concerning this teaching.

Vatican I, reaffirmed in Vatican II,[34] taught that the Pope as head of the College of Bishops and Successor of Peter has the same infallibility that is guaranteed to the Church. When the whole Church is united in a belief as being revealed truth, it cannot be in error. This was the principle enunciated by Augustine and so important to Newman in his *Essay on the Development of Christian Doctrine,* "Securus iudicat orbis terrarum" (The judgment of the whole world is certain).[35]

Infallibility does not guarantee that a papal definition is prudent, wise, or timely. It does not guarantee that the arguments used to support the definition are cogent or even cor-

---

[32] Schatz, *Papal Primacy*, 153.

[33] Ibid., 154.

[34] Dogmatic Constitution on the Church (*Lumen Gentium*) §18. See above, chapter 1, n. 6.

[35] See *Corpus Scriptorum Ecclesiasticorum Latinorum*, vol. 34 (Vienna: F. Tempky, 1895), epist. Parmen. III, 4; 24.

rect. The prerogative of infallibility guarantees only that what is defined is *true*.[36] Newman, for instance, was quite emphatic in his belief that the definition of papal infallibility was not wise or prudent. For one thing, he felt that it would create an insurmountable obstacle to conversion to the Catholic Church. But, interestingly, he also believed that it would be practically impossible to express the truth about infallibility with sufficient accuracy in words, and that once defined it would lead to endless debates about whether this or that utterance of the Pope was infallible.[37] This has proved to be the case also because Vatican I did not treat of the ordinary Magisterium of the Pope. As a result, for many (including some theologians), even the ordinary Magisterium took on the quality of infallibility.[38] It should be clear, however, that Newman himself held the doctrine of papal infallibility. He simply thought that it was not prudent or opportune to define it.

Furthermore, Catholic doctrine holds that papal infallibility occurs through divine *assistance,* not through inspiration. This means that papal infallibility does not come about because the Pope receives some kind of supernatural illumination or vision or that he has some personal endowments of insight or intuition not given to others. Papal infallibility comes about through the Providence of God over the Church, which means that the Pope must take all the humanly avail-

---

[36] See, e.g., Sixtus Cartechini, S.J., *De Valore Notarum Theologicarum* (Rome: Gregorian University Press, 1951), 22–23; Francis A. Sullivan, S.J., *Creative Fidelity* (New York: Paulist Press, 1996), 33–40.

[37] See John R. Page, *What Will Dr. Newman Do? John Henry Newman and Papal Infallibility* (Collegeville, Minn.: Liturgical Press, 1994), p. 66, §7, p. 71.

[38] See Yves Congar, *Eglise et Papauté* (Paris: Editions du Cerf, 1994), 279. The Pope exercises the ordinary Magisterium in encyclicals, apostolic exhortations, and other documents directed to the whole Church. Also, when he gives explicit, formal approval to doctrinal statements of the Congregation for the Doctrine of the Faith. See Francis A. Sullivan, S.J., *Magisterium* (Dublin: Gill & Macmillan, 1983), 189–52.

able means to discover the truth and is obligated to weigh the prudence of proceeding to a definition.[39]

But the definition of papal infallibility, the reverence for and focus on the person of the Pope, and increasingly strong centralization by the Vatican have all tended to expand the idea of divine assistance into a kind of continuing divine inspiration. This mystique, which has come to surround and engulf the Pope especially since the nineteenth century, creates a deep psychological barrier to speaking in critical terms about policies, declarations, or actions of the Pope. For instance, there are divergent views about the procedures relating to the evaluation, questioning, and condemnation of the writings of theologians,[40] about the policies of Rome in dealing with episcopal conferences, about the procedures for the appointment of bishops. Since these belong to the class of administrative or policy decisions, there is no virtue nor any principle of faith or reason that would prohibit a variety of viewpoints on such topics. But there is great reluctance on the part of many Catholics and especially bishops to say anything negative for fear of offending against the reverence due to the papal office. Reverence for the Pope, then, is another factor that reinforces resistance to criticism in the Church.

The Media: A Modern Cause of Resistance to Criticism

In addition to the two causes for resistance on the part of Church leaders to criticism already mentioned (reverence for

---

[39] Vatican Council I, "First Dogmatic Constitution on the Church of Christ (*Pastor Aeternus*), chap. 4, in *Decrees of the Ecumenical Councils,* ed. Tanner, 2:816. See also Sullivan, *Magisterium,* chap. 5, "The Infallibility of the Magisterium in Defining Dogmas of Faith" (pp. 79–118). An example of theological thinking before Vatican II is Timotheus Zapelena, S.J., *De Ecclesia Christi, Pars Altera* (Rome: Gregorian University Press, 1940), 79.

[40] See, e.g., Gerald O'Collins, S.J., in *The Tablet,* December 12, 1998, p. 1650.

the Pope, and fear of contributing to attacks on the Church), one should add a third cause: the negative impact from the way the media often handles these issues. This resistance comes out of the pastoral concern of Church leaders and their obligation to prevent scandal. The legitimate pastoral concern to prevent scandal is rooted in the Gospel itself, where Our Lord in the strongest language declares, "Woe to the world because of scandals" (Matt. 18:7). The pastoral ideal has always been to contain what is scandalous so that the faith of the many is not injured and the mission of the Church is not compromised. The fact that the media, especially the modern electronic media, bring information instantly to all parts of the world deepens these pastoral concerns of the Church.

The problem becomes more acute when the media, reporting doctrinal or moral teaching, may frequently fail to report it fully or accurately. This too creates great pastoral concern precisely because a false, distorted, or incomplete version of official teaching can be spread with such impact all over the world almost instantly. Journalists can sensationalize stories, fail to make the necessary distinctions or to place them in perspective, and even be irresponsible and unprofessional in reporting.

The media itself acknowledges its flaws. For instance, in June 1998, CNN and *Time Magazine* jointly charged that the United States had used nerve gas to kill defectors during the Vietnam War. But on July 2, they retracted the story. An editorial in the *New York Times,* listing some of the reasons for this turnabout, commented:

> [B]arracks gossip, and unreliable reconstituted memories all were stretched into a dramatic but unproven charge . . . . they did not have enough evidence to make such explosive charges. Most important, they were so intent on proving their case, they did not listen closely enough to the many sources who insisted that their premise was not true.[41]

---

[41] "The CNN-Time Retraction, *New York Times,* July 3, 1998, p. A16.

The editorial goes on to report similar failures in journalistic standards on the part of the *Boston Globe*, the *New Republic*, and the *Cincinnati Enquirer*. Two professional journalists in a recent work entitled *Warp Speed* decry the media for its loss of professional standards and ethics, for the developing lack of concern for verification, the growing power of sources over journalists, and their dependence on pseudo-experts and pseudo-facts. The new mixed-media culture is creating "what we call a new journalism of assertion, which is less interested in substantiating whether something is true and more interested in getting it into the public discussion."[42] These examples, dealing with reporting of secular stories, serve to show why Church leaders can be critical of the media and resistant to making known what may be critical of the Church. Few journalists, except for some connected with the major media, have any real training in theology or religious topics. While most media would not assign a journalist to cover sports events who had no knowledge of sports or to cover politics who had no knowledge of politics, there is no hesitation in assigning journalists to cover religious stories who have no knowledge of religion, of religious language, or of Church structures and history. None of this should obscure the fact that there are extremely competent, fair, and responsible journalists who, even—and perhaps especially—when they are responsibly critical, perform an invaluable service to society, to the Church, and to freedom.[43]

See also Gustavo Gorriti, "Where Journalists Still Get Respect," *New York Times,* July 21, 1998, op-ed page A19. Also "Journalists Probe Their Own Credibility Gap," *San Francisco Chronicle,* August 1, 1998. Whatever is to be said about the attitude of Church leaders to the media, these stories show that the media itself recognizes that it does not always perform up to standard and that a negative attitude by the clergy is not just pique or narrow-mindedness.

[42] Bill Kovach and Tom Rosenstiel, *Warp Speed* (New York: Century Foundation Press, 1999), 8.

[43] In my personal experience over the years I have been impressed by

But antagonism between the Church and the media is not new, nor does it derive exclusively from egregious failures to meet the best standards of journalism. It is related also to a strain of anti-Catholic and anti-religious bias of some media both in editorial policy and in reporting and is another reason for the reluctance to encourage criticism from within the Church. Throughout the nineteenth century the press, particularly in France and Italy, had a particular hostility to the Catholic Church. This hostility was due to various causes. The papacy was a political power, ruler of the Papal States, and an actor in the political life of Europe. The papacy tended to be on the side of established political authority, which further incited the hostility of those elements seeking change. The press, on the other hand, was greatly influenced by the political and philosophical currents of the age—rationalism, pragmatism, skepticism, and relativism. It was hostile to the idea of religious authority, to revelation, and to the supernatural. All these factors underlay the European press's attacks on the beliefs and practices of the Church and on the policies of the Holy See. They also underlay the vigorous anticlericalism of the press. In this context it is somewhat understandable that Church leaders would be negative.

Pius VII, for example, in 1814 protested to Louis XVIII against freedom of the press in France with the observation that the press was, "the principal instrument which has,

---

such reporters as Kenneth Briggs, formerly with the *New York Times,* and Peter Steinfels, also with the *New York Times.* These reporters understood the issues they were reporting on, knew what questions to ask, and reported stories in a balanced way and accurately. I cannot now recall all the journalists, print and television, I have dealt with over more than thirty years. I have met others like those I mentioned above. I have also met those who did not have even the most limited understanding of Church matters. One television reporter who had scheduled an interview with me after I returned from an international synod in Rome asked when I entered the room, "What are you here to report on?" Ignorant of why I was at the studio, he had no knowledge or understanding of Church matters or teaching.

first, depraved the morals of the people, then corrupted and destroyed their faith, and finally, stirred up seditions, troubles and revolts."[44]

But the problem of a Church hostile to the press was not confined to Europe. "Because of strident, often-partisan American journalism in those days [i.e., in the nineteenth century], the U.S. bishops became frozen in an attitude that the press was hostile to Catholicism."[45] In the United States in the nineteenth century the Catholic Church was largely an immigrant Church. There was a strong measure of hostility toward immigrants, especially those who did not speak English, like the Polish and Italians, and English-speaking immigrants, like the Irish, who were not Protestant. This prejudice was shared by the press.

It would be a mistake to think that prejudice against the Catholic Church existed only in the nineteenth century. It is in the twentieth century that the distinguished historian Arthur Schlesinger said that the deepest bias in the American people is the anti-Catholic bias.[46] This was shown a few years ago in tolerant San Francisco. A respected theater was considering performing a play in which a white actor, using blackface, played the part of an African-American. The decision was made to abandon that play on the grounds that it would be offensive to African-Americans if a white actor played an African-American. Another play was chosen. The second play, called "The Pope and the Witch," portrayed the Pope as a drug dealer who becomes demented, and a nun as aiding a group of young people in acquiring drugs. No thought was given to the grave offense such a play was to Catholics. Enormous efforts, public and private, were made

---

[44] Cited by Richard N. Ostling, *Secrecy in the Church* (New York: Harper & Row, 1974), 81.

[45] Ibid., 84–85.

[46] Andrew M. Greeley wrote compellingly about twentieth-century anti-Catholicism in *An Ugly Little Secret* (Kansas City, Kans.: Sheed Andrews & McMeel, 1977).

to persuade the director to abandon this play, but nothing could move her and the play went on. Billowy rhetoric appeared about free speech, the narrowess of the Catholic Church, and its efforts to impose its views on San Francisco.

Things like this have naturally contributed to the negative attitude of church leaders to the media and are another reason for their resistance to criticism within the Church. Does the legitimate pastoral concern for accuracy in reporting doctrinal matters and for preventing scandal and the weakening of faith justify widespread secrecy and lack of cooperation with the media today?

Secrecy: One Way of Containing Criticism

Whatever may have been true in past times, we have to face the fact that in today's world few things can be kept confidential indefinitely. If the policy of the ecclesiastical authorities is to withhold information, to give as little information as possible, and for the most part only to react, the possibility of presenting a story in an accurate and balanced way is lost. This defect cannot adequately be made up by later efforts to clarify or correct distortions but will create the impression in the public mind that something has been concealed, that there has been a lack of honesty, and the credibility of the Church suffers. For example, a month after his election, Pope John Paul I died suddenly and unexpectedly in 1978. The Vatican delayed announcing the death for many hours and reported that the Pope died reading a medieval spiritual work called *The Imitation of Christ*. Later it was revealed that the story about reading the spiritual book was not true. The delayed announcement and the fabricated story about what the Pope was doing when he died, together with the failure to hold a full inquiry about the circumstances surrounding the pope's death, only served to reinforce suspicions of foul play and weakened later attempts to explain and clarify the story.

An Official Policy of Openness

Ironically, six years before the death of John Paul I, the Vatican published a document on communications dated January 29, 1971. About secrecy it says this: "When ecclesiastical authorities are unwilling to give information or are unable to do so, then rumor is unloosed, and rumor is not a bearer of truth but carries dangerous half-truths."[47] Journalists who cannot get truthful information from informed sources will get information where they can find it. In a thoughtful discussion of secrecy, journalist Richard Ostling wrote more than twenty years ago:

> Secrecy is impossible. Information will get out eventually, so the choice is between a timely, full, accurate, honest, useful report available to everyone; and a distorted, inaccurate hearsay account which gets to some people much earlier than others.[48]

Another difference from the past is that in the world of modern journalism "deadline" has a new meaning. Journalists no longer work only in the context of a morning or evening paper or radio or television broadcast. In this electronic age, reporting is worldwide and is going on twenty-four hours a day, and stories are broadcast minutes after they occur. This heightens the importance of honest and informed sources supplying the information. When inadequate information is given or inquiries by the media are met with no response, when the story finally does go out, there will be need for clarifications. The pressures under which modern journalists and news organizations work only reinforce the importance of cooperation if only out of motives of

---

[47] "Pastoral Instruction on the Means of Social Communication" (January 29, 1971), §121, in *Vatican Council II: The Conciliar and Post Conciliar Documents,* ed. Austin Flannery, O.P. (Northport, N.Y.: Costello, 1975).

[48] Ostling, *Secrecy,* 13–14.

self-interest. Secrecy and noncooperation are not effective responses to the actual or perceived faults of the media. Nor are they a means today of preventing or limiting criticism within the Church.

Pope John Paul II and Criticism

Pope John Paul II touches on the place of criticism in the Church today when he says, "Acknowledging the weaknesses of the past is an act of honesty and courage which helps us to strengthen our faith, which alerts us to face today's temptations and challenges and prepares us to meet them."[49]

These words might lead us to believe that it is sufficient to acknowledge the weaknesses of the past, that present realities which merit criticism are not included. But he goes on to say:

> Many Cardinals and Bishops expressed the desire for a serious examination of conscience above all on the part of the *Church of today....* An examination of conscience must also consider the *reception given to the Council....* [I]s the ecclesiology of communion described in *Lumen gentium* being strengthened? (*Tertio millennio adveniente* §36)

These questions indicate a consciousness on the part of the Pope that there are problems in the Church of today and that chief among the objects of such an examination of conscience is the reception being given to the Second Vatican Council and to the ecclesiology of communion. An examination of conscience implies the willingness to face up to what is wrong, even sinful, to admit it, and to take steps to correct it. Such an honest examination of conscience cannot be one-sided. All sons and daughters of the Church are

---

[49] Encyclical letter on the approach of the third millennium (*Tertio millennio adveniente*), November 10, 1994 (Vatican City: Libreria Editrice Vaticana, 1994), §33.

called by the Pope to this examination of conscience. An examination of conscience means criticism.

A striking example of contemporary criticism within the Church is the Cardinal Prefect of the Congregation for the Doctrine of the Faith, Joseph Ratzinger. In a book of personal reminiscences, Cardinal Ratzinger described the decision of Pope Paul VI to forbid the further use of the preconciliar rite of the Mass as the introduction of "a breach into the history of the liturgy whose consequences could be only tragic."[50] This criticism is significant, coming as it does from one of the most important members of the papal curia and directed against a recent Pope. It is surprising also that it was made not in closed circles but in a published and widely read work.

Another example of contemporary criticism within the Church comes from Bishop Reinhold Stecher of Innsbruck, Austria, whose criticism of the Pope and of curial policies received widespread publicity.[51] One-fifth of the priests of Austria gave their signature to Bishop Stecher's declaration.[52] With the growing decline of priests in mind, and speaking of the Vatican decree on lay ministers, Bishop Stecher said:

> My real concern is the refusal to recognize the actual pastoral situation in so many countries the world over and the refusal to recognize the theological importance of the Eucharist. . . . The Decree on Lay Ministers is concerned entirely with defending the rights of the ordained. It shows no concern for the health of the community. For some time now we have been offering people, tacitly but in reality, a non-sacramental way of salvation. Those familiar with scholastic theology can only shake their heads in disbelief. For that theology strongly

---

[50] Cardinal Joseph Ratzinger, *Milestones* (San Francisco: Ignatius Press, 1998), 148.

[51] *The Tablet,* February 28, 1998, p. 291.

[52] "The Church in the World," *The Tablet,* March 14, 1998.

emphasizes the necessity for salvation of the Eucharist, penance, and anointing of the sick.[53]

These examples of criticism in the contemporary Church come from individual bishops. Another example, however, comes from a more collegial criticism expressed on November 21, 1998, by the bishops of New Zealand in an audience with Pope John Paul II.[54] Their statement has the merit of both respect and honesty but definitely conveys the sense that these bishops have a consciousness of their own responsibility for the Church—in their communion with the Pope. The spokesman, Bishop Cullinane, said:

> Exactly 20 years ago I was privileged to be among the crowd in St. Peter's Square the hear the announcement of your election. Now I and my brother bishops welcome the opportunity to assure you of our unaffected loyalty to your office and to yourself personally.

After thanking the Pope for his leadership and his important writings, which he calls "prophetic," the bishop went on to say:

> We in turn would not wish to be like those false prophets who sought their own advantage by telling people that everything was well. Nor would it be in the spirit of the Apostles Peter and Paul for us to speak less than honestly about our concerns for the Church.

Speaking in the name of the bishops of New Zealand, Bishop Cullinane then pointed out several instances of inconsistency in the action of Rome. He recalled the Pope's request for discussion about the exercise of the primacy and how it contrasts with the action of the Curia making norms with little or no consultation with the episcopate. He mentions the declared intention of preserving the proper freedom of the

---

[53] *The Tablet,* March 14, 1998.

[54] See Peter James Cullinane, "A Time to Speak Out," *The Tablet,* November 28, 1998, p. 1589.

Eastern Catholic Churches alongside the policy of evicting their priests from Latin dioceses or not permitting them to be ordained in Latin dioceses. There are, he says, the assurances that faith cannot be imposed on anyone alongside the threat of penalties for those who have difficulty with "teachings that the Church does not teach definitively." He noted the Pope's call for the ecclesial community to foster the gifts and responsibilities of women in the Church. But he observed that this has not really happened. "We . . . consider the matter urgent, because only when that happens will people see that equality does not depend on Ordination."

These examples serve to illustrate that modern criticism of the Church does not come only from uninformed, disaffected, or malevolent sources. Cardinal Ratzinger, Bishop Stecher, and the bishops of New Zealand have served the Church faithfully and consistently over a lifetime. It is also an illustration that side by side with an official resistance to criticism there exists a continuing expression of criticism even from highly placed sources within the official structures.

Public Opinion: A Necessary Form
of Criticism Today

Not only are prominent church leaders themselves publicly critical, there is a body of church teaching supportive of public criticism under the name of *public opinion.*

Pope Pius XII (1939–1958) was the first Pope to use the expression "public opinion" in relationship to the Church. He said:

> Public opinion is part of the legacy of any normal society constituted of human beings. . . . We wish to add a word about public opinion in the Church, in those matters that are open to free discussion. The expression of such opinion comes as a surprise only to those who do not know the Catholic Church, or who have a false opinion of it. For the Church, too, is a living organism, and an important element

would be missing from its life were it to be without expression of public opinion. The blame for this shortcoming would lie with its shepherds and faithful.[55]

Fifteen years after these words of Pius XII, Vatican II took up the theme of public opinion. The council declares,

> [W]hile observing the moral order and the common benefit, people should be able to seek the truth freely, to express and publicize their views, to cultivate every art, and finally they should be informed of the truth of public affairs.[56]

To avoid the conclusion that this freedom exists only in the secular realm, the council explicitly applies the same thought to the Church: "It should be recognized that the faithful, clerical as well as lay, have a just freedom of inquiry, of thought and of humble and courageous expression in those matters in which they enjoy competence" (*Gaudium et Spes* §62)

When this text was debated in the council, an amendment was submitted calling for the deletion of the word "courageous." This amendment was rejected with the terse response that "courage is not without value."[57] Humble expression, yes. But courageous—not timid or fearful. We should note also that this "just freedom of inquiry, of thought and of humble and courageous expression" is the prerogative of all members of the Church—"clerical as well as lay."

Seven years after the council, the Holy See published a lengthy document on communications which declares that public opinion in the Church is not merely a right but a necessity:

---

[55] See *L'Osservatore Romano,* February 18, 1950.

[56] Constitution on the Church in the Modern World (*Gaudium et Spes*), §59, in *Decrees of the Ecumenical Councils,* ed. Tanner, 2:1110.

[57] "Fortitudo non est inutilis"; see *Commentary on the Documents of Vatican II,* ed. Herbert Vorgrimler (New York: Herder & Herder, 1968), 5:287.

Since the Church is a living body, she needs public opinion in order to sustain a giving and taking between her members. Without this she cannot advance in thought and action. . . . Catholics should be fully aware of the real freedom to speak their minds which stems from a "feeling for the faith" and from love. . . . Those who exercise authority in the Church will take care to insure that there is responsible exchange of freely held and expressed opinion among the People of God. . . .

Since the development of public opinion within the Church is essential, individual Catholics have the right to all the information they need to play their active role in the life of the Church.[58]

It is clear that these principles apply not only to individuals. The document goes on:

The normal flow of life and the smooth functioning of government within the Church require a steady two-way flow of information between ecclesiastical authorities at all levels and as organized groups. This applies to the whole world.[59]

The official documents of the Church, then, call on Church authority to encourage and elicit public opinion, which means that there must be an atmosphere conducive to public opinion in the Church. Public opinion in the Church means that people can plainly express what they are feeling and thinking "with real freedom to speak their minds." The endorsement of public opinion, of course, is an endorsement of criticism in the Church.

Public opinion and the criticism which it implies are necessary for Church authority to carry out its responsibilities. Church leaders—especially the Pope, bishops, and pastors—cannot prudently lead unless they know the actual situation, which includes knowing what people think. They have to

---

[58] "Pastoral Instruction on the Means of Social Communication," §§115–17, 119, in *Vatican II,* ed. Flannery, 330–36.

[59] Ibid., §120.

know the hopes and dreams of the people, what their problems are, what they find difficult and why. Karl Rahner
points out that the greater the number and diversity of people involved, the more difficult it is to know the situation
and therefore the greater need for public opinion.[60] That certainly describes the situation of the Church today—the great
diversity within the Church, the immense numbers.

What led Pius XII and Vatican II to bring up the issue of
public opinion? A powerful factor behind this was the experience of the Pope himself and many bishops under the totalitarian regimes of the World War II period.[61] One of the
marks of these regimes was the control and suppression of
public opinion. Pius XII and the council did not want the
Church to be tainted by appearing to be a totalitarian regime
marked by the absolute control and suppression of public
opinion within her own sphere of life.

Conditions and Limits
to Public Opinion in the Church

Public opinion, as described in Church documents, cannot
be restricted only to the expression of agreement with the
institutional Church.[62] A doctrinal reason why there can be
a legitimate public opinion that is not in agreement with certain kinds of positions or policies of Church authority is that
the life of the Church is guided not only by the Pope and
bishops, though it remains always under their direction, but
by the action of the Holy Spirit. As Rahner says, the Holy
Spirit "can breathe upon whomsoever he will in the
Church—even the poor, the children, those who are 'least in
the Kingdom of God'—and infuse his own impulses into the
Church in ways that no one can foretell."[63]

---

[60] See Karl Rahner, *Free Speech in the Church* (New York: Sheed &
Ward, 1959), 22.

[61] Ibid., 17.

[62] Ibid., 18.

[63] Ibid.

This mention of "the children" is reminiscent of the great *Rule* of St. Benedict, which requires that in important matters, the abbot must consult all the monks because "the Lord often reveals what is better to the younger" (chap. 3).

Does this official support for public opinion mean that there is an open field, that members of the Church can adopt and promote any position whatsoever? Endorsement of public opinion must mean that there are some areas open to divergent views. Such things as policy or administrative decisions of the Pope and bishops would fit this category. But ours is a revealed religion. There are other areas which, if you *freely* choose to be a member of the Church you *freely* accept as true. When people are baptized they are entering a universal community of faith that already exists, and they embrace the faith of that community as handed on by the apostles.[64] But even in this doctrinal area there is room for the change which is development. The Council of Ephesus, for instance, though its doctrinal affirmations were true, was inadequate and needed the Council of Chalcedon to bring further clarity and focus to its teaching. Even in the realm of defined truth it is necessary to distinguish between the truth that is taught and the adequacy of its expression and its concepts. To maintain that a certain way of expressing a revealed truth is inadequate or that the concepts in which it is understood are inadequate in no way implies a denial or lack of Catholic faith. In fact, Newman wrote: "[O]ne cause of corruption in religion is the refusal to follow the course of doctrine as it moves on, and an obstinacy in the notions of the past."[65]

---

[64] Faith means fundamentally the acceptance of the self-revelation of God and a surrender to God in his only Son, Jesus Christ. But that faith can and must also be put into words, propositions. In baptism, the new member of the Church is embracing Jesus Christ but also the propositions or statements of faith that are held by the community of faith, the Church. For more on this topic, see Sullivan, *Magisterium*, 12–14.

[65] John Henry Newman, *An Essay on the Development of Christian*

The first freely chosen limit on criticism and public opinion, then, is made up of those things which are divinely revealed and held by the Church, the community of faith. Members of the Church cannot reject the word of God, dogmas of the faith taught by the Church, the divinely willed constitution of the Church and her apostolic structure, or the sacraments. Given the apostolic constitution of the Church, the definitive determination of what is divinely revealed truth belongs to the apostolic office in the Church, that is, to the College of Bishops of which the Pope is at once member and head.

In this connection, Karl Rahner makes an important point: "But the Church cannot be a debating society; it must be able to make decisions binding on all within it."[66] And he adds:

> Even a Church with open doors is not a fair where each and every opinion can set up a stall. It remains true that the Church can have the right and duty to declare authoritatively and unambiguously that this or that doctrine cannot be put forward in the Church as Christian or Catholic.[67]

Clearly, then, according to the teaching of the Church, there is a place for public opinion, freely, humbly, and courageously expressed, in the Church. On the other hand, it is equally clear that those who enter the Church embrace the faith of the Church which places limits on public opinion and diversity of views.

Criticism of the Pope in the Church

Because it has become such a sensitive point, it is important to return here to the issue of criticism of the Pope from

---

Doctrine (Westminster, Md.: Christian Classics, 1968) chap. 5, section 1, §8, p. 177.

[66] Karl Rahner, *The Shape of the Church to Come* (New York: Seabury Press, 1974), 54.

[67] Ibid., 74–75.

within the Church. A classic instance of criticism in the Church is the public criticism of the first of the apostles by the last of the apostles recorded in Galatians 2:11–14. Paul describes it this way:

> But when Cephas [Peter] came to Antioch, I opposed him to his face, because he stood self-condemned; for until certain people came from James, he used to eat with the Gentiles. But after they came, he drew back.... But when I saw that they were not acting consistently with the truth of the gospel, I said to Cephas before them all, "If you, though a Jew, live like a Gentile and not like a Jew, how can you compel the Gentiles to live like Jews?"

In Paul's view, Peter has given scandal and misled even Barnabas. Whatever is to be said about this incident, it clearly witnesses that in principle the chief of the apostles is not above criticism, at the very least by the other apostles, and that he is not above public criticism.

What about the relationship of the bishops and the Pope today? Is there room for criticism? The future cardinal, Joseph Ratzinger, in his earlier writings, opens up an interesting line of thought. He points out that the relationship of the bishops with the Pope cannot be confined within a narrow juridical perspective. There is also the level of the human, moral interaction between bishops and Pope. He says:

> Now among the claims which his very office makes upon the Pope we must undoubtedly reckon a moral obligation to hear the voice of the Church universal.... Juridically speaking, there is no appeal from the Pope even when he acts without the college, and the college cannot act without him at all; morally speaking, the Pope may have an obligation to listen to the bishops, and the bishops may have an obligation to take the initiative themselves.... The Council of Constance serves to remind us of this truth and also of the limitations of juridical formulae.[68]

---

[68] Joseph Ratzinger in *Commentary on the Documents of Vatican II,*

For the bishops to "take some initiative" would certainly include their making known their criticisms to the Pope.

The distinction made here by Cardinal Ratzinger between the moral and juridical levels is one of great significance. Thus, within the College of Bishops there is not only a "hierarchical" element by reason of which the Successor of Peter is head of the college and has certain prerogatives in virtue of which the bishops are said to be *sub Petro* (under Peter). There is also an element of reciprocity and mutuality in virtue of which there is room for a certain initiative on the part of the bishops in relationship to the head of the college: the bishops are *cum Petro* (with Peter). This initiative must include the possibility of the bishops pointing up certain deficiencies or areas where change or adaptation is needed in the Church. In other words, there is a place for criticism on the part of the bishops.

In the modern world it is simply not possible to believe that all the bishops of the world are in agreement with every administrative or policy decision of the Pope. To attempt to create the illusion of unanimity or even consensus where it does not exist and cannot exist is to run the risk of diminishing the moral authority and credibility of the Church. To portray all criticism and disagreement as disloyalty or lack of faith is a grave injustice.

There are those who say that criticism in general, and in particular criticism of the Pope, has potential to be misunderstood, even to give scandal. Speaking of the avoidance of criticism because it might cause scandal, St. Augustine said:

> One must therefore tell the truth, especially when a difficulty makes it all the more urgent that the truth be told. Let those grasp it who can. Far be it that, in keeping silence out of consideration for those who might not be able to understand,

---

ed. Vorgrimler, 1:304. See also J. Grootaers, *Primauté et Collégialité: Le dossier de Gérard Philips sur la Nota Explicativa Praevia* (Leuven: Leuven University Press, 1986), 43–44.

not only truth be frustrated, but those be left in error who could have grasped the truth and thus escaped their error. . . . How fearful we are that the truth may harm those who will not be able to understand! Why are we not afraid that if we remain silent, those who could have understood will be deceived. (*De Bono Perseverantiae,* chap. 16)

St. Thomas raises the issue of criticism not in terms of permissibility but in terms of obligation: Is one *obliged* to correct a superior? (*Summa Theologiae* II-II, q. 33, a. 4). He begins by pointing out that correction is an act of charity. Charity must extend, he says, to all persons, and therefore it must extend to superiors. Though Thomas does not explicitly mention him, this would surely include the Pope. According to Thomas, in general everyone, priest or lay person, can be obligated to offer correction even to the Pope, since the Pope must be an object of charity. Thomas goes on to argue that since any virtuous act must be shaped and moderated by the circumstances involved, correction of superiors by their subordinates must be done in an appropriate way, that is, without arrogance or harshness, but with gentleness and reverence. He quotes the Letter to Timothy, "And so the Apostle says in his First Letter to Timothy, 'Do not upbraid an older man, but appeal to him as a Father'" (1 Tim. 5:1).

In addition, Thomas makes specific reference to the fact that an equal can publicly correct a superior, and he uses precisely the example of Paul correcting Peter (*Summa Theologiae* II-II, q. 33, a. 4, ad 2). Thomas further cites Augustine to the effect that in this instance Peter left an example to those in authority that should they stray from the right path, they should not resist being corrected by others. He goes on to point out that in this instance Paul was the equal of Peter because both had the same obligation to defend the faith and it was in his upholding the faith that Peter was defective. Ordinarily public correction of a superior exceeds the bounds of fraternal correction, but it can be done even by a lay person when the faith is in jeopardy (ibid.).[69] What this shows is that for Thomas no superior is in principle beyond correction by either equals or subordinates.

Qualities of Criticism in the Church

If criticism in the Church is to be constructive and evangelical, what are its ideal qualities? Criticism in the Church is, of course criticism made by a disciple in the Church. As such it should be under the Spirit and should have the characteristics of all action under the Spirit which are described in the Letter to the Galatians: "the fruit of the Spirit is love, joy, peace, patience, kindness, faithfulness, gentleness and self-control. . . . If we live by the Spirit, let us also be guided by the Spirit. Let us not become conceited, competing against one another, envying one another" (Gal. 5:22–23, 25–26).

Constructive criticism is motivated by the desire to improve the Church, to enable it to fulfill its mission more effectively. This kind of criticism is offered with consideration and respect, with faith and charity and the other qualities mentioned in Galatians. But given the criticisms such as those of St. Bernard and St. Catherine, constructive criticism in the Church can also be forthright, bold, and courageous. Destructive criticism, on the other hand, is often divisive, intemperate, competitive, blind to a larger vision, and without reverence for authority. For Aquinas, correction of a superior should be characterized by reverence, respect, moderation, and charity for the person corrected.

When it is a question of criticism of the Church, there must be a real love for the Church rooted in a mature Catholic faith. Karl Rahner, speaking of the failings and even oppression experienced within the Church at times, calls on

---

[69] "ubi immineret periculum fidei, etiam publice essent praelati a subditis arguendi." Here Thomas does not explicitly use the word "lay person"; he uses the word "subject" (*subditus*). But, of course, the greater number of "subjects" of prelates would be lay persons.

the Catholic to recognize and admit these failures and defects, but he insists:

> [A]ttachment to the Church must be part also of the spirituality of the future. Otherwise it [criticism] is elitist arrogance and a form of unbelief. . . . Attachment to the Church will, also in future, be an absolutely necessary criterion for genuine spirituality.[70]

Our faith is not just in an abstraction, a Platonic ideal. We believe in the Church in its concrete historical reality, that is, with its strengths and weaknesses, its divine endowments and human defects. "The dream of a *papa angelicus* leads away from reality now just as it did in the Middle Ages."[71] Raymond Brown once observed that we never cease to be scandalized that God has placed the mystery of salvation in human hands. (This observation was made during a day of prayer for priests in San Francisco by Fr. Brown in the early 1990s.) And so Rahner rightly calls for a genuine submission to the actual representatives of the Church with their actual human limitations, faults, and sins. He says:

> Catholics who want to take a real share in the development of public opinion within the Church must live like true Christians and make the Church's cardinal mysteries the basis of their personal life. It is only possible to combine this right sense of proportion about Church matters with the ability to share, calmly and constructively, in the development of a public opinion within the Church—. . . without resentment or bitterness or any indulgence in backbiting—if one is really in touch with the vital sources at the heart of the Church's supernatural activity.[72]

---

[70] Karl Rahner, *Concern for the Church* (New York: Crossroad, 1981), 153.

[71] Schatz, *Papal Primacy*, 178. The expression *papa angelicus* means "angelic pope." It comes from the prophecies of Nostradamus, who gave various names to future popes. Pius XII was referred to as "angelic shepherd."

[72] Rahner, *Concern for the Church*, 42–43.

In other words, the evangelical critic is at the same time a true disciple, living the life of faith and charity, eyes fixed on Christ crucified, risen and glorious.

Criticism and Patience

The evangelical critic must have evangelical patience. Those who love the Church must suffer for the Church. They must often, as well, suffer from the Church. A distinguished scripture scholar, Carlo Martini, makes the same point:

> All those situations which at first sight seem incomprehensible and unacceptable to us—when the cry rises within us: anything, but not this!—are in fact the ones that place us at the heart of the manifestation of the mystery of God.[73]

One who suffered greatly from the Church and who nevertheless loved the Church greatly was the French theologian Yves Congar. His monumental work *True and False Reform in the Church,* when it appeared in the early fifties, was ordered out of seminary and other Catholic libraries and its further sale was proscribed.

Congar speaks of receiving an unceasing series of denunciations, warnings, and mistrustful interventions from Rome for a period of nine years.[74] He was required to submit all

---

[73] Carlo Maria Martini, *Promise Fulfilled: Meditations,* trans. Alan Neames (Middlegreen, Slough, U.K.: St. Paul's, 1994), 85. Carlo Martini, S.J., now archbishop of Milan, served for many years on the faculty of the Biblical Institute in Rome, of which at one time he was also Rector. He is a co-editor of the Greek New Testament published by the United Bible Societies.

[74] See Yves Congar, *Dialogue Between Christians,* trans. Phil Loretz, S.J. (Westminster, Md.: Newman Press, 1966), 34. An interesting story circulating during the fall of 1963, the second session of Vatican II, was the rumor that Cardinal Antoniutti of the Roman Curia had sent a letter to the superiors general of some of the religious orders warning them against certain experts at the council, among them Yves Congar, Karl Rahner,

his writings to Rome, even short book reviews.[75] It is worthy of note that one factor which created suspicion about his and other theologians' writings was that they were using the sources—scripture and the fathers. This uneasiness about the sources seems to mark the maximalist line of interpretation of Vatican I, which continues today in the restorationist and anti-Vatican II movements, which themselves seem so little rooted in the sources.

Congar's personal suffering in the Church—and from the Church—in this and subsequent instances gives immense credibility to his words. Having observed that evangelical patience means that those who suffer in the Church must have the courage not to deny in the darkness what they have seen in the light,[76] he goes on to say:

> [Patience] is a certain quality of mind, or rather of soul, which takes root in these profound convictions: first, that God deals the cards and fulfills in us his plan of grace; second, that for great things, certain delays are necessary for maturation. . . . Those who do not know how to suffer no longer know how to hope. . . . If the patience is that of the sower, it must be accompanied by the Cross. "Those who sow in tears, reap in song," but at times they do not reap at all for "it is one who sows and another who reaps." The cross is the condition of every holy work. . . . Only through the cross do we ourselves achieve authenticity and depth of existence. Nothing is worth doing unless one agrees to pay the price.[77]

Hans Küng, and Joseph Ratzinger. See Henri Fesquet, *The Drama of Vatican II* (New York: Random House, 1967), 197.

[75] Congar, *Dialogue Between Christians,* 40.

[76] The context would indicate that he does not here mean a determined clinging to one's own views, but rather that "in the light" one has seen the beauty of the Church, her divine character, Christ, the glory of his sacred passion and death, and when in darkness because of the Church, does not deny these realities, rooted in Christ, who "is the same yesterday, today, yes, and forever."

[77] Yves Congar, "The Need for Patience," *Continuum* 2, no. 4 (Winter 1965). Also in Congar, *Dialogue Between Christians,* 44–45.

Authentic evangelical critics are conscious of their own shortcomings. Humility is a necessary quality of criticism in the Church. The Lord commands that we first be aware of the plank in our own eye before turning attention to the speck in the eye of another:

> Why do you see the speck in your neighbor's eye, but do not notice the log in your own eye? . . . You hypocrite, first take the log out of your own eye, and then you will see clearly to take the speck out of your neighbor's eye. (Matt. 7:3–5)

Surely there is nothing more incongruous than an arrogant disciple of a Lord who washed his own disciples' feet.

Criticism, according to the Gospel, must be just. It must relate to facts and not be exaggerated. Its purpose must be to build up the Church. It is not revenge or retaliation. Criticism in the spirit of discipleship rests on the power of God and not on worldly power and force.

> [A] demand for this reform must come not by way of systematic disobedience, manipulation, hostility, or "ecclesial terrorism," but in the sole strength of the Word, and of the element of truth contained in each word of that Word.[78]

Neither reform nor criticism, then, is foreign to the Church or to the papacy. Criticism per se is not excluded within the Church, nor is it necessarily a manifestation of disloyalty or weak or defective faith. On the contrary, both Pope Paul III in anticipation of the Council of Trent and Pope John Paul II in the pursuit of Christian unity took the initiative and explicitly asked for criticism—John Paul II, for criticism of the exercise of the primacy with a view to its reform. Pope Paul VI embodies the Church's encouragement of and openness to criticism in these words to the Roman Curia:

> We have to accept criticism with humility and reflection and admit what is justly pointed out. Rome has no need to be defensive, turning a deaf ear to observations which come

---

[78] González Faus, *Where the Spirit Breathes,* preface, p. xiv.

from respected sources, still less, when those sources are friends and brothers.[79]

Any serious effort to respond to Pope John Paul II's invitation to enter into dialogue with him concerning "a way of exercising the primacy . . . open to a new situation" will necessarily involve some criticism. The following chapters attempt to make just such a response, and to make it in the framework and spirit described here.

---

[79] Pope Paul VI, "Address to the Roman Curia, September 21, 1963," *AAS* 55 (October 12, 1963): 797. *AAS* is the acronym for *Acta Apostolica Sedis* (Acts of the Apostolic See). This is a kind of "Congressional Record" of the Vatican. It contains all official decrees, speeches of the Pope, and papal encyclicals and is considered the official record.

CHAPTER 3

The Papacy and Collegiality in the Church

In chapter 1 we saw that Pope John Paul II pointed to the collegial structures of the first millennium as a model and guide for Christian unity today (*UUS* §55). Since Christian unity involves communion with Rome (*UUS* §97), central to any realistic hope of unity is a real and more than symbolic collegiality within the Catholic Church itself. The way the Pope exercises his primacy in relationship to the rest of the College of Bishops in the Catholic Church will naturally be taken as an indication of how he would exercise the primacy in regard to the Orthodox episcopate and others, such as the Anglicans, in the event of full communion with Rome.[1] If they see an exercise of the primacy which seeks to diminish the collegiality of the bishops or make it inconsequential, this will pose a serious obstacle to unity. The Orthodox have preserved from the pre-Nicene Church the synodal, collegial structures of the Church, and the Orthodox canons stress the structural importance of synods and participative episcopal government.[2]

And so, to pursue the quest of Christian unity, it is necessary to raise the question: Can the role and authority of the

---

[1] See my Oxford lecture "The Exercise of the Primacy," *Commonweal,* July 12, 1996, section 1, p. 12.

[2] Notwithstanding the official stance of the Orthodox in regard to the synodal structure of the Church and the clear articulation of this in their canons, in practice an individual hierarch may appear to be acting in a highly authoritarian way. I will return to this point in chapter 4.

bishops be affirmed without threatening or weakening the primacy?[3] How would the fuller affirmation of the role and authority of the bishops create a new situation for the primacy that would make it healthier for the Church?

The Primacy Expanded

The Pope's primacy can be weakened in two ways. One is by so exaggerating the role of the episcopate that the Pope becomes a mere executor of the will of the majority. The other is the inflation of the role of the Pope. For example, Rome's fear of criticism by the Reformers led to an overemphasis on secrecy and the need to defend everything. This, in turn, fed into the tendency of some to expand divine assistance—the ground of papal infallibility—into inspiration or divine illumination casting an aura of infallibility on almost everything the Pope says or does. When this happens the credibility of papal authority is diminished.

This position was present in Vatican I and is called the "maximalist" interpretation of papal primacy. While this position was not the teaching of Vatican I or of its definition of primacy, it was in the air, so to speak, and has continued from that time to this in segments of the Roman Curia and elsewhere in the Church.[4] Yves Congar points out that Vatican I was silent about the ordinary Magisterium of the Pope. As a result, many devout Catholics and some theologians held that all papal teaching was infallible.[5] The extreme exaltation of papal teaching even held that there was a sort of incarnation of Christ in the Pope, almost two "real presences," the real presence of the silent, hidden Christ in the Eucharist and the real presence of the teaching, visible Christ

---

[3] For a well-developed treatment of this question, see Michael J. Buckley, S.J., *Papal Primacy and the Episcopate* (New York: Crossroad, 1998).

[4] Hermann J. Pottmeyer, *Towards a Papacy in Communion* (New York: Crossroad, 1998), 104–9.

[5] Yves Congar, *Eglise et Papauté* (Paris: Editions du Cerf, 1994), 279.

in the Pope.[6] While this point of view never developed a following of consequence, it had a certain quiet influence at various levels.

The maximalist position at Vatican I held that there is only one teacher in the Church, the Pope. Consequently, the bishops are basically hearers and passive receivers of papal teaching and decisions. There is no need for the Pope to consult with the episcopate about Church teaching or even in the definition of dogma. Hermann Pottmeyer points out how such a point of view leads to creeping, or as he puts it, "galloping" infallibility and blurs the lines between what is of faith and other papal pronouncements. The maximalist position also identified primacy of jurisdiction with primatial sovereignty.[7]

Bismarck and the German Bishops

While the official teaching of Vatican I did not embody this maximalist position, in much of the popular mind it did. A celebrated and instructive instance of this occurred two years after Vatican I when Bismarck, Chancellor of the German Empire, addressed a confidential message to all the German diplomatic representatives in which he informed them that the teaching of Vatican I on the Pope's primacy of jurisdiction "appropriated to the Pope episcopal rights in each diocese and substituted pontifical jurisdiction for that of the bishops

---

[6] See Jean-Marie R. Tillard, *L'Eglise locale* (Paris: Editions du Cerf, 1995), 498 n. 2.

[7] See Pottmeyer, *Towards a Papacy,* 51–75. An example of what some understood as papal sovereignty is described by Henri Maret, nineteenth-century dean of theology at the Sorbonne. Maret, opposing the idea of papal sovereignty over the Church, says that papal sovereignty would mean that there is nothing in the Church in addition to or above the Pope. It is indivisible because it excludes any participation whatever in the government of the universal church. It is unlimited because the Pope is answerable only to God. Maret's anaysis of sovereignty is set forth in Pottmeyer, 57.

of the country."[8] This message remained confidential for two years until it appeared in an official government publication in connection with the trial of a German diplomat in 1874.[9]

As soon as the Bismarck document became known, the German bishops reacted quickly and vigorously. They published a forthright statement in February 1875. In it they denounced the Bismarck communiqué as erroneous and lacking foundation. They specifically stated that the decrees of Vatican Council I offer no basis for the position that the Pope has become an absolute sovereign.[10] Speaking of the role of the bishops in the Church, they said, "We can decisively refute the statement that the bishops have become by reason of the Vatican decrees mere papal functionaries with no personal responsibility."[11] They added: "According to this teaching of the Catholic Church the pope is bishop of Rome, not bishop of any other city or diocese, not bishop of Cologne or of Breslau."[12]

They explicitly affirmed that the Pope cannot absorb the role of the episcopate, that the episcopate exists by divine institution as does the primatial office, and that this is the constant teaching of the Church through the centuries and of the ecumenical councils of the past. The Pope cannot change this divine constitution of the Church. With equal clarity, however, the German bishops explicitly acknowledged the primacy of jurisdiction of the Pope: "As bishop of Rome, he is at the same time pope, i.e., pastor and supreme head of the whole Church—head of all the bishops and faithful."[13]

Pius IX made two responses to this important statement.

---

[8] See F. Donald Logan, "The 1875 Statement of the German Bishops on Episcopal Powers," *The Jurist* 21 no. 3 (July 1961): 286.

[9] Ibid.

[10] Ibid., 290.

[11] Ibid., 291.

[12] Ibid., 292.

[13] Ibid., 289.

The first, a letter addressed to the German bishops in which he praises them and states his agreement with their teaching:

> You, venerable brothers, have certainly continued this glory of the Church by undertaking the restoration of the germane sense of the Vatican definitions against the distortions made in the captious comments of the recently published Circular-Dispatch. . . . Your statement is indeed so clear and sound that, since it leaves nothing to be desired, We ought to content Ourselves by merely giving you Our fullest congratulations. Due to the pernicious clamor of some journals, however, a more solemn approval is required . . . your statement does give the original Catholic teaching, and, moreover, the teaching of the Sacred Council.[14]

This letter was dated March 2, 1875. Less than two weeks later, Pius IX followed up on his words that "a more solemn approval is required." At a consistory creating eleven new cardinals, the Pope said:

> The merciful God who presides over and counsels His Church, has providently directed that the very brave and courageous bishops of the German Empire by their illustrious statement, which will remain memorable in the annals of the Church, have with supreme wisdom refuted the erroneous teachings and sophistries put forward on this occasion, and, having erected a noble monument to truth, have given joy to Us and to the Church universal. . . . Their remarkable declarations and protestation, which are worthy of the courage, the office, and the piety of such men, we ratify and in the exercise of the fullness of Our apostolic authority do hereby confirm.[15]

Thus, Pius IX himself on two public occasions emphatically rejected the Bismarck position and authoritatively confirmed that the statement of the German bishops was the

---

[14] Pius IX, *Mirabilis illa constantia,* March 2, 1875, in *Enchiridion symbolorum, definitionum et declarationum de rebus fidei et morum,* ed. H. Denzinger, rev. A. Schönmetzer (36th ed.; Freiburg: Herder, 1976), no. 3115.

[15] Logan, "1875 Statement," 295.

authentic teaching of the First Vatican Council itself. Thus understood, it is a statement that the primatial office is not an absolute monarchy. As the episcopate must recognize the prerogatives inherent in the primatial office, so the pope must recognize the prerogatives inherent in the episcopal office. Nor does the primacy of jurisdiction mean continual and direct intervention by the Pope in the responsibilities of the bishops: "[T]he Pope is bishop of Rome, not bishop of any other city or diocese, not bishop of Cologne or of Breslau."[16]

Cardinal Newman, while accepting the definitions of the First Vatican Council, was among those who recognized that its teaching, since it did not deal in a more developed way with the role of the bishops, was incomplete and would have to be balanced by some future council. In fact, he saw this balancing of previous councils by later councils as a pattern of history: "Rather he looked forward eagerly, almost with defiance, to a new pope and a new council. . . . A new council was needed to set things right, to put the definition in its proper perspective."[17] Paul VI mentioned this in his opening address at the second session of the council. He pointed out that John XXIII, by the fact of calling a council, repudiated the erroneous interpretation of Vatican I according to which, given the infallibility and the primacy of jurisdiction of the Pope, ecumenical councils were no longer necessary. This idea that councils were unnecessary implied that the Pope of himself possessed everything needed for the teaching of the faith and the government of the Church and that the episcopate was inconsequential. Paul VI went on to state explicitly that Vatican II was necessary in order to repair, complete, or restore what was lacking (*resarcire*) in Vatican I.[18]

---

[16] Ibid., 289.

[17] John R. Page, *What Will Dr. Newman Do?* (Collegeville, Minn: Liturgical Press, 1994), 408–9.

[18] Address of Paul VI, September 29, 1963; see *Constitutiones, Decreta, Declarationes* (Vatican City: Typis Polyglottis Vaticanis, 1966), 900. See also Charlton T. Lewis and Charles Short, *A Latin Dictionary* (New York: Oxford University Press, 1962), s.v., *resarcio*, p. 1576.

Roman Centralization and Collegiality

Because of the readiness with which many have inflated the teaching of Vatican I, and the fact that notwithstanding the *doctrinal* clarifications of Pius IX, the centralizing tendency of the papacy continued unabated under Pius IX and during the century since Vatican I, it is not surprising that with the coming of the Second Vatican Council in the 1960s, the bishops of the world became convinced that the high centralization wrought by Rome had to be balanced by a clear teaching on the collegiality of the episcopate and that the *practice* of the Church had to be brought into line with that teaching.[19]

But it was not only the episcopate of the world that recognized this need, it was felt even at high levels of the Roman Curia. Archbishop Giovanni Benelli, when Substitute Secretary of State, observed:

> The real, effective power of jurisdiction of the Pope over the whole Church is one thing. But the centralization of power is another. The first is of divine law. The second is the result of human circumstances. The first has produced many good things. The second is an anomaly.[20]

Primacy of jurisdiction does not render the episcopate nugatory or simply a passive recipient of papal decrees and dispositions, neither of itself does it mean centralization of power.

It is critical to recall Pius IX's vigorous support of the statement of the German bishops because today the maximalist position at Vatican I, even though repudiated by Pius IX, still exists, and there is a tendency to bypass the episcopate in the belief that there is only one real bishop in the Church, the Pope. There is an unexamined frame of mind that the primacy of jurisdiction means that the Pope can at any moment

---

[19] See Pottmeyer, *Towards a Papacy,* 110–24.

[20] Giovanni Benelli, "Les rapports entre le Siège de Pierre et les Eglises locales," *Documentation Catholique* 70, no. 1644 (December 16, 1973), cited in Congar, *Eglise et Papauté,* 28.

and for whatever reason intervene in the affairs of any diocese or even of any parish. This is the mentality that identifies primacy with sovereignty and regards the desire for a truer collegiality in the Church as a plot to take power from the Pope and "turn the Church into a democracy."[21] But the rooted, measured language of Pius IX and of the German episcopate enshrine the convergence of primacy and collegiality affirmed in balanced tension, neither doing injury to the other. Neither the papacy nor the episcopate stands alone. Both exist and function within one and the same reality, which is called the College of Bishops. Each exists in communion with the other. This authentic interpretation of Vatican I was rooted in the tradition of the fathers and the history of the first millennium. The maximalist interpretation did not think it necessary to have recourse to the fathers and ignored the first millennium.[22] It is interesting that the absolutizing and centralizing policies of Gregory VII in the eleventh century, as we will see, were also weak in knowledge of the patristic heritage, especially the Eastern fathers, and of the first millennium.

The fact is not that the bishops of Vatican II sought to diminish the papal office, but that they were more aware of the history of the first millennium and of the fathers, which enabled them to see that the dogmatic decrees of the First Vatican Council concerning the Pope, which they embraced and reaffirmed (*Lumen Gentium* §18), were incomplete and in that sense one-sided. Vatican I had established the parameters, as the statement of the German bishops proved, but it did not close the debate or solve all the problems.[23]

---

[21] See, e.g., the editorial by Robert Moynihan in the periodical *Inside the Vatican*, August–September 1996. It would be interesting to examine why such commentators take such a negative view of the introduction of what they call "democratic" factors into the Church, while they do not take a negative view of the introduction of other secular "monarchical" factors into the Church.

[22] See Pottmeyer, *Towards a Papacy*, 51–75.

[23] See Vatican Council I, *Pastor Aeternus*, chap. 3, in *Decrees of the*

Collegiality: The Minority Opposition at Vatican II

When it finally convened in the fall of 1962, the Second Vatican Council had a membership of some 2,100 bishops from all over the world. This number varied a bit from one day to another because of deaths, new appointments, and absences. Of this number, about three hundred bishops were opposed to the doctrine of collegiality and, when they saw that it would be taught by the council, did everything possible to limit it. They were a small but important minority.

Behind the opposition of this minority lay a monarchical idea of the papacy greatly influenced by the maximalist position of Vatican I. Many in this group were members of the Roman Curia, and a large number were canonists and so had a heavily juridical idea of collegiality. Their understanding of collegiality came from classical Roman law.[24] They were negative about applying the idea of collegiality to the episcopate because in Roman law a college was an aggregate of equals. The members of the college possessed equal and coordinate authority subject to mutual control. But what these bishops seemed unable to recognize was that collegiality as discussed in the council did not derive so much from Roman law as from the practice of the Church during the first millennium.[25]

Ecumenical Councils, ed. Normon P. Tanner, S.J. (New York: Sheed & Ward; Washington, D.C.: Georgetown University Press, 1990), 2:813–14. Not only is the role of the bishops affirmed, but Vatican I teaches that it is the role of the Pope to affirm, strengthen, and vindicate the role of the bishops. In other words, Vatican I teaches that the Pope is not simply to tolerate the bishops' role; he is actively to promote their role "a supremo et universali pastore asseratur, roboretur ac vindicetur . . . ." This is made much more explicit in the confirmation by Pius IX of the statement of the German bishops. See above, pp. 78–81.

[24] See *The Oxford Classical Dictionary,* ed. N. G. L. Hammond and H. H. Scullard (2nd ed.; New York: Oxford University Press, 1970), s.v. *collegium,* p. 264.

[25] Both Francis A. Sullivan and Patrick Granfield have pointed out that the word "collegiality" is not found in *Lumen Gentium,* the Vatican II Dogmatic Constitution on the Church. One possible explanation for this

Some also believe that this minority did not have a correct understanding of the dogmatic decree *Pastor Aeternus* of Vatican Council I. That council, though incomplete in its teaching about the bishops, was not altogether silent about their role. It did teach that the Pope has a primacy of jurisdiction, but it went on to situate that primacy within the episcopate and to show that the primacy exists first for the unity of the bishops and, with and through them, for the unity of all the faithful.[26]

Since the sixteenth century, and especially since Vatican I, so much emphasis has been placed on the role of the Pope that the actual, carefully nuanced teaching of *Pastor Aeternus* has been obscured not only in the popular mind but even in the minds of many bishops. In fact, "[t]he way *Pastor Aeternus* has been distorted in its reading has influenced ecclesiology for almost one hundred years."[27] This limited and incomplete grasp of Vatican I was another factor that shaped the negative attitude of the minority toward collegiality at Vatican II. It is also a factor that underlies the vocal opposition of some today to any mention of a true and functional collegiality.

Development of the Doctrine of Collegiality at Vatican II

The articulation of the doctrine of collegiality taught at Vatican II went through several stages. When Pope John XXIII announced in January 1959 that he was convoking a council, committees were established to do the preparatory work. The Committee on the Doctrine of Faith and Morals, headed by

---

is that classical Latin, in which the decree was written, does not have the word *collegialitas*. But the Latin text of *Lumen Gentium* does have the expression *ratio collegialis* (chap. 3 n. 22). This would seem to me to be the classical Latin equivalent of *collegialitas*.

[26] Buckley, *Papal Primacy and the Episcopate*, 45–52.

[27] Ibid., 45.

Cardinal Ottaviani, pro-Prefect[28] of the Holy Office (later called "The Congregation for the Doctrine of the Faith") over a period of two years prepared a draft document on the Church for consideration by the future council. When the council actually assembled, this draft was discussed for six days, from December 1 to 7, 1962.[29] Ultimately, though there was no formal vote, it was set aside as being too scholastic and juridical—inadequate. This draft did not reflect the vision and emphasis of Pope John's opening address to the council, in which he called for new ways of expressing Catholic doctrine and for the avoidance of harsh condemnatory language.

During the months prior to the council's first session, several groups had been working informally on their own version of a possible document on the Church. And when the official document was set aside, one of these drafts, called the Belgian draft,[30] was accepted by the working committee as the basis for a new attempt. Working from this draft, a second, official draft document was presented to the council for deliberation in the fall of 1963. Though more acceptable than the first draft, this draft too required much more work. When the session ended in December 1963, the Theological Com-

---

[28] Prior to the revisions brought about by Vatican II, the Pope himself was Prefect of the Holy Office. Hence the title "pro-Prefect" used at that time for Cardinal Ottaviani.

[29] This draft was unsatisfactory for a number of reasons: too scholastic, too juridical, not pastoral. An objection to it raised by Cardinal Montini (soon to be Pope Paul VI), by other Latin Church bishops, and by Eastern patriarchs was that the draft seemed to be an unrelated series of disparate topics; it lacked sufficient internal coherence. The draft consisted of eleven chapters, the first of which, revealing the tone of the document, was "The Nature of the Church Militant." See Gérard Philips, "Dogmatic Constitution on the Church, History of the Constitution," in *Commentary on the Documents of Vatican II*, ed. Herbert Vorgrimler (New York: Herder & Herder, 1968), 1:106.

[30] This draft was sometimes referred to as the Philips draft or the Suenens draft. See André Naud, *Un aggiornamento et son eclipse* (Montreal: Fides, 1996), 46.

mission began the work of preparing a third draft in light of the discussion on the council floor and of the amendments that had been presented.[31]

All the while, Pope Paul VI was very much aware of the strong opposition of the minority to collegiality, some of whom, because of their curial background, had ready access to him.[32] He was very much concerned to avoid a stalemate in the council and wanted to exert every effort to bring about a consensus.

A sign of his own personal preoccupations and in an effort to make things more acceptable to the minority, Paul VI sent to the Theological Commission a series of thirteen proposed amendments, which he said were meant as suggestions. In its plenary session in June 1964, the commission considered these suggestions. Among them, three are of particular interest to the consideration of collegiality.[33] One suggestion was that a phrase should be inserted into the text stating that the Pope is "answerable only to God." The commission rejected the suggestion, pointing out that the Pope is bound by the ethical demands of the gospel, by justice, by the dogmatic decrees of previous councils, by the divine structure of the Church, by the sacraments, and "by too many other things to mention." The commission thus situated the papacy clearly within the Church and affirmed certain limits on papal authority. An important point for the Orthodox is the binding character of the canons of the ecumenical councils. For them it is important that the Pope show that he regards himself as bound by and observes the provisions of the canons.[34]

---

[31] Philips, in *Commentary on the Documents of Vatican II,* ed. Vorgrimler, 1:105ff.

[32] Paul VI worked in the Vatican Secretariat of State from 1924 to 1954. Thus, he would have known many of those in the minority group who had also worked in the Curia.

[33] See J. Grootaers, *Primauté et Collegialité* (Leuven: Leuven University Press, 1986), 135–39.

[34] See E. Ghikas, "Comment 'redresser' les définitions du premier con-

A second suggestion of Paul VI was that the Pope should be called "Head of the Church." The commission also rejected this as open to misunderstanding. Christ is the Head of the Church. The Pope could be called the visible head of the Church, but to insert this expression it was felt would only cause needless ambiguities. The title "Head of the Church" could give the impression that the Pope was outside and above the Church.[35]

A third suggestion was that the text should state that the Pope has full, supreme, and universal power in the Church, "which he can always and freely exercise." The Theological Commission, although it accepted the suggestion, dropped the "and" in "always and freely," making the text read, "he can always freely exercise." The commission gave as its reason for this that otherwise the impression would be given that the Pope could arbitrarily and continually intervene in the pastoral government of the bishops.[36] By these decisions, the commission upheld the role of the episcopate and at the same time affirmed that papal authority has limitations, some of a divine nature, some of a prudential nature.

One of the great ecumenical concerns today and an obstacle to Christian unity, is the fear that the Pope can arbitrarily intervene in the affairs of local or regional churches and that he does in fact do so. For instance, the repeated rejection by Rome of decisions made by the Episcopal Conference of the United States is interpreted by many Orthodox, Anglicans, and Protestants as an indication of "what it would be like" if they entered into full communion with Rome. These repeated acts of rejection of the decisions of an entire episcopate constitute in their view a witness that collegiality in the Catholic Church is merely symbolic. Ecumenically such actions go far to undermine what the Pope has said in the encyclical *Ut unum sint*. Actions speak louder than words.

---

cile du Vatican," part 2, "La Primauté de juridiction," *Irénikon* 68 no. 2 (1995): 182–204.

[35] Grootaers, *Primauté*, 137–38, §9.

[36] Ibid., 136, §6.

Paul VI's Personal Views on Collegiality

Some hold the view that Paul VI, while he supported the majority position on collegiality, was not himself entirely comfortable with it. Grootaers explicitly says:

> It became clear to those who worked on the commission [the Doctrinal Commission] that Paul VI wanted to safeguard at all costs the complete monarchical power as it existed before him and which he felt the obligation to preserve for his successors.[37]

In a personal conversation with J. Grootaers in 1969, four years after the council, Gérard Philips, who had been Undersecretary of the Doctrinal Commission at the council, said that Paul VI could not internalize the idea of collegiality—he always thought of himself as outside the council.[38]

This appraisal of a learned and experienced theologian such as Gérard Philips, who was known for his prudence and reserve, must carry a certain weight. Yet it must also be balanced by the fact that Paul VI did submit his proposals to the Theological Commission of the council as "suggestions" and not as commands, and that he did do everything in his power to prevent a rejection of collegiality by the minority.

Though he did support the movement toward a greater actual collegiality of the episcopate,[39] Paul VI was also concerned about any weakening of the papal office as defined at Vatican I. It is reported that during the debate on collegiality he spent many nights studying the question to make sure that what was taking shape did not quarrel with the papal powers as defined in Vatican I.[40]

That Paul VI had this personal sense of papal tradition is also borne out by a personal experience I had with him. In the

---

[37] Ibid., 32.

[38] Ibid., 33.

[39] *Commentary on the Documents of Vatican II*, ed. Vorgrimler, 1:127.

[40] See Peter Hebblethwaite, *Paul VI: The First Modern Pope* (New York: Paulist Press, 1993), 384–92.

early 1970s, I was chairman of a subcommittee of the Bishops' Conference dealing with medical ethics in Catholic hospitals. A committee made up of doctors, nurses, hospital administrators, and theologians from different parts of the country met approximately every two months with me to discuss ethical problems in medicine and in hospital policy. The discussion would frequently bring up the problem of tubal ligation in Catholic hospitals and under what circumstances it became a forbidden form of contraceptive sterilization. Despite frequent discussion of the issue, the committee was unable to reach any consensus. The problem was very serious because there were at the time at least seven hundred Catholic hospitals in the United States. I made a personal survey of the position of moral theologians and in particular of those teaching in the Roman universities at the time. The theologians did seem to be largely of a more open frame of mind in regard to permitting tubal ligation, and this raised the question whether their position constituted a probable opinion.[41] If a probable opinion could be established, Catholic hospitals could authorize tubal ligations in a wider range of situations.

I presented the problem to the Administrative Committee of the Bishops' Conference, and the bishops agreed that the matter was serious and needed resolution. Consequently it was decided that the officers of the conference, under the presidency of Cardinal John Krol,[42] would go directly to the

---

[41] "Probable opinion" is a technical expression used in moral theology meaning that a position has enough backing by experts that it can be applied in practice.

[42] At the time archbishop of Philadelphia. In addition to Cardinal Krol, the group consisted of Cardinal Cooke of New York, Bishop Bernard Flanagan, of Worcester, Massachusetts, and Bishop James Rausch, General Secretary of the Bishops' Conference. At a social gathering a few days after our meeting with Paul VI, Archbishop Giovanni Benelli, then the chief official of the Secretariat of State after the Cardinal Secretary, sought me out and expressed thanks for having brought the problem of the hospitals to the Pope's attention.

Pope and that I would accompany them and present the matter for his consideration. Materials had been sent in advance, and these together with the oral presentation enabled the Pope to have a good understanding of the problem as we confronted it in the United States. After listening carefully to what I had to say, Paul VI remarked that he could see how serious the problem was and what far-reaching implications it had and that he would give it very careful consideration and ask the Congregation for the Doctrine of the Faith for its advice. But he concluded, "I hope you can understand my problem, too. I feel deeply the weight of the teaching of my predecessors." It was clear he was greatly preoccupied about upholding the continuity of papal teaching.

A major effort of Paul VI to support collegiality while accommodating the resistance of the minority as well as his own preoccupations was what is called the "Prefatory Note."[43] It was a preface to a report by the Theological Commission on how it had handled amendments to the document on the Church on which the council had already voted. The note, contained in a dossier given to the council fathers, is not an act of the council, was never a part of the council document on the Church, and was never voted on by the council. But when it was announced in the council that "higher authority" had directed that this Prefatory Note be given to the fathers, and that the teaching contained in chapter 3 of *Lumen Gentium* was to be explained and understood according to the mind and sense of this note, everyone understood that "higher authority" meant the Pope. This showed that the Pope was extremely anxious, by offering the clarifications contained in the note, to reassure the minority and to avoid a rupture or a large negative vote. The Pope was quite successful in his aim. At the final vote on November 21, 1964, there were only five negative votes. The council—the bishops united with their head, the Pope—accepted and taught the doctrine of collegiality.

---

[43] See *Decrees of the Ecumenical Councils,* ed. Tanner, 2:899–900.

Further Clarifications of the Prefatory Note

It is mildly surprising to find Archbishop Pietro Parente among the first to speak in defense of the final document on the Church. Archbishop Parente was a well-known Roman theologian, at one time professor and Rector of the Propaganda Fide College. During the council he was the Theological Commission's reporter to the council and at the same time an official in the Holy Office.[44] It would have been expected that he would be aligned with Cardinal Ottaviani and with the minority opposition group. But according to Parente, all the points made in the Prefatory Note are contained in the text of the council document. In other words, the council document on the Church was not a one-sided promotion of collegiality. He stated that the note simply gave a certain emphasis or explanation but did not add anything substantial to the text. "This Note," he said, "pleased the Pope and by his direction it was brought to the Council hall. But the vote of the Fathers was not on the Note. It was on the text of the Constitution" (i.e., on the Dogmatic Constitution, the document on the Church).[45] Later, as a cardinal, Parente repeated his defense of the text of the council,

> As far as the important point about the primatial power of the Roman Pontiff, the Constitution [i.e., the council document on the Church] upholds it vigorously and unequivocally even without the Note. This is why I unhesitatingly wrote that the Note could be called useful in some sense, but not necessary.

Others close to the process stated the same position.[46]

---

[44] He was Assessor of the Holy Office. In general terms, this is a consultative or advisory function which has some distant foundations in Roman law where private citizens were called on to advise on matters under dispute. The Latin name is *adsessor,* that is, one who sits nearby so as to be able to give advice. For more on this, see Gregory Girard Ingels, "Assessors in the Judicial Tradition of the Church" (diss., Faculty of Canon Law at the University of St. Thomas, Rome, 1987).

[45] Grootaers, *Primauté,* 45.

[46] Ibid., 45–46.

Gérard Philips commented:

> [T]he Prefatory Note had as its purpose to attenuate the reservations held by a certain number of Latin bishops [i.e., those of the Latin as distinct from the Eastern Churches] who tended to read [into collegiality] a threat against the primacy of the Pope. The final text tried to take into consideration all points of view from whichever source they came. But the result was, because of numerous corrections, a certain heaviness. The Constitution itself breathes freely of the mentality of communion; the Prefatory Note, is primarily concerned with juridical precautions.[47]

There can be no doubt what the mind and intent of the council was then. The majority, the pro-collegiality group in the council, was concerned to avoid two risks. Having explicitly professed the teaching of the First Vatican Council, it opposed any interpretation of collegiality that would make the Pope simply an executor of the will of the episcopate. It equally and vigorously opposed any reading of the text that would situate the Pope beyond or outside the Church or make him an absolute monarch. The council did not want to teach so inflated a doctrine of papal primacy as to support the maximalist interpretation of Vatican I and diminish or make the collegiality of the episcopate superfluous.

The Primacy in the First Millennium

The ancient practice of the first-millennium Church of bringing *causae maiores,* major issues, to the Pope very early indicates a sense that the bishop of Rome has a unique and ultimate authority among the Churches and their bishops. But that power was not exercised on a daily basis. It was rare and exercised with moderation and measure for the greater good of the Churches. During the first thousand years, the exercise of the primacy appears especially in conjunction with an ecumenical council. Since one of the chief purposes of the

---

[47] Ibid., 51–52.

primacy is the unity of the bishops, it is fitting that it emerges
at those moments of doctrinal crisis when their unity is especially required by the Church.

It is not surprising, then, that the Orthodox position on the
centralizing and interventionist policies of the reform movements of the eleventh century under Leo IX and especially
Gregory VII is precisely that it was discontinuous with the
history of the previous thousand years. As two respected
Orthodox authors put it, "Pope Gregory's theories and logic
were seriously flawed and equivocal. And of course both his
actions and arguments lacked historical precedent."[48] They
continue:

> It is worth repeating again that the men responsible for this
> fundamental "discontinuity" were initially almost all mem-
> bers of the German episcopate. The aggressive self-confidence
> which inspired them, as we have seen, was rooted in the
> northern monastic reform movement. They were heirs to
> Carolingian theology and civilization. As "ultramontane"
> churchmen they were often at the same time uninformed of
> the papacy's ancient Mediterranean orientation. . . . [S]uch
> regrettable innocence explains their determination to extend
> everywhere the direct right of intervention of the papacy—
> even in the East where the Churches had enjoyed a good deal
> of autonomy in running their internal affairs according to
> their own custom. . . . Like their Carolingian forerunners,
> certainly the Gregorians were for the most part unaffected by
> ancient ecclesiology or by the Greek patristic tradition.[49]

Congar is of the opinion that while after 1054 (the date tra-
ditionally associated with the break between Rome and Constantinople) there were contacts and even signs of existing
communion, nevertheless there is justification for the view
that this date symbolically marks the moment when the eccle-
siologies of the East and the West went their separate ways in

---

[48] Aristeides Papadakis and John Meyendorff, *The Christian East and
the Rise of the Papacy* (Crestwood, N.Y.: St. Vladimir's Seminary Press,
1994), 53.

[49] Ibid., 55–56.

growing ignorance of the other.[50] The expansion of the role of the Pope in the West proceeded without the balancing influence of the Greek patristic tradition and without the ecclesiological traditions of the Eastern Churches. Because of this, both the Catholic Church and the Eastern Churches experienced an impoverishment. A narrowing of consciousness took place. The great horizons shaped by a living communion of East and West had slipped away into the shadows.

It is true that in the tenth and eleventh centuries the Western Church suffered from very serious evils calling for strong leadership. Chief among them were simony, the buying and selling of episcopal appointments, of monasteries, of the cardinalate; lay investiture, the control by civil powers over the appointment of bishops, abbots, and other sacred offices; lay patronage, the control by the civil powers or by wealthy lay persons over churches and their priests. As was to be expected in such a situation, the pastoral care of the people was greatly diminished. Preaching was at a low ebb, as was the sacramental life of the people.

One aspect of the problem was the generally low standard of the clergy:

> The fragmentary evidence of institutions in England before 1250 suggests that some 80 percent of those appointed rector had not yet been ordained priest. They were pressed to proceed to the priesthood as soon as possible and to reside in their benefices, but even if they did so it remains true that bishops who were endeavoring to build up the pastoral ministry were normally obliged to appoint men without experience, who had never presided at Mass, heard a confession or preached a sermon.[51]

Reform was certainly needed, but this could not happen unless the Church freed itself from lay and royal control. The

---

[50] Yves Congar, *L'Eglise de Saint Augustin à l'époque moderne* (Paris: Editions du Cerf, 1996), 99–100.

[51] Colin Morris, "The Papal Monarchy," in *The Oxford History of the Christian Church* (Oxford: Clarendon Press, 1991), 537.

evils of the time indeed called for vigorous and decisive action on the part of the Pope. Because of this, the monarchical idea of the papacy grew in emphasis during the Renaissance period, and its influence lingered in various ways until the collegiality debate at the Second Vatican Council, which did not completely end this frame of mind.

Typology was invoked in support of the monarchical idea. The earthly church was a reflection of the heavenly, in which God is unique and supreme. Hence, there had to be in the earthly church a monarchical structure reflective of this heavenly reality.[52] Perhaps the earliest proponent of this approach was Peter Damian (d. 1072), who drew his idea from the book of Revelation: the heavenly city Jerusalem descending from God.[53] Fidelity to the typology required a supreme head ruling over all.

In their appeal to typology, these reform figures failed to give sufficient weight to the eschatological character of their biblical types. They failed to attend to the difference between what marks the Church in her earthly pilgrim state from what will mark her in the future prepared by God when Christ will come again in his glory. They failed to give sufficient attention to the structures of the Church as they appear in the New Testament, where Peter, though first among the apostles and their head, is not apart from the College of the Apostles to which the mission of grace and salvation has been entrusted.

In addition to the love of typology, Gregory VII and the Gregorian reformers placed emphasis on the image of the Church as the Body of Christ nourished by the Eucharist. As a result, they placed the priesthood at the center of all hopes for reform and the papacy at its head.[54]

Gregory differed from previous reformers in his emphasis on law and on the consequent doctrine of the Pope as the fountainhead of all Church law. The whole Church thus

---

[52] See John W. O'Malley, S.J., *Praise and Blame in Renaissance Rome* (Durham, N.C.: Duke University Press, 1979), 220ff.

[53] Congar, *L'Eglise de Saint Augustin*, 93.

[54] Ibid., 102–22.

becomes totally dependent on the papal monarchy. And with this the foundations have been laid for a juridical ecclesiology dominated by the papacy. It is easy to see how in this line of thinking obedience to the Pope became one of the preeminent marks of true faith.

Congar mentions how the Gregorians commonly thought of the Church as one immense diocese, so large that the Pope could not deal with it alone and as a result he set up vicars or surrogates who to some degree shared his power—the episcopate.[55] It is this theological-juridical ecclesiology which naturally led to the great centralization that the Catholic Church has experienced from that time to this.

The vigorous and decisive monarchical, juridical centralization of Gregory VII and his successors was not due to a passion for self-aggrandizement. It was due, on the one hand, to the lack of a broader grasp of the patristic tradition and to the impoverishment resulting from separation from the Eastern Churches. It was due also to the determination of good men to free the Church from the destructive control of civil rulers and lay patrons. Some Orthodox and other Christians and even some within the Catholic Church, look upon this monarchical, centralizing development as irreversible and believe that Rome thinks of this high centralization as an unrenounceable feature of the papal office. Yet an examination of the situation shows that these were historical provisions made in view of a given situation and can be changed. As Pope John Paul II has pointed out in *Ut unum sint,* the papal office is one thing and the way it is exercised is another (*UUS* §95).

In promoting episcopal collegiality, was the majority at the Second Vatican Council promoting an egalitarian model of papal authority? By no means. They had explicitly reaffirmed the definitions of Vatican I. Moreover, they were extremely careful to articulate the doctrine of collegiality at the same time as they affirmed a true primacy: the head of the College

---

[55] Ibid., 105.

of Bishops has certain prerogatives that the other members of the College do not have. But that is not the same as absolute monarchy, nor, of course, is collegiality the same as undifferentiated democracy. Vatican Council I was not in error. It was incomplete and it needed clarification.

The Basis for the Vatican II Teaching on Collegiality

On what, then, did Vatican II base its teaching about collegiality? First the Council addressed the question of the sacramentality of the episcopate. For centuries in the West, there had been different schools of thought. For instance, both St. Albert the Great and St. Thomas held that the episcopate was not a sacrament. But since the Council of Trent the great majority of theologians have held it to be a sacrament and the Second Vatican Council explicitly affirmed that the episcopal office is conferred through a sacrament properly so called: "This sacred Synod teaches that by episcopal consecration is conferred the fullness of the sacrament of orders" (*Lumen Gentium* §21).[56]

Based on this doctrinal truth, the council teaches that one becomes a member of the College of Bishops through sacramental ordination: "[I]t devolves on the bishops to admit newly elected members into the episcopal body by means of the sacrament of orders" (*Lumen Gentium* §21). This, of course, means that the College of Bishops is constituted not by a juridical act but by a sacrament, by the fullness of the sacrament of Holy Orders. The collegiality of the bishops is not the result of the decision of a council, or of a provision of canon law, or of the decision of a Pope. Collegiality is a property of the sacramental nature of the episcopal office. The

---

[56] See above, chapter 1 n. 6. In order to witness to this doctrinal truth after the council, the word "ordination" was substituted for "consecration." It is interesting that in recent years the word "consecration" is making a return in what are sometimes called "restorationist" circles.

College of Bishops is constituted by Christ, who, sent by the Father and acting through the Holy Spirit, is the minister of the sacrament.[57] Inasmuch as the Pope is a bishop through episcopal ordination, he is irrevocably a member of the College of Bishops and can never be placed outside it. So true is this that canon 332 directs that if a person who is not a bishop is elected Pope, he is to be ordained immediately inside the conclave and does not have the powers of the Pope until he is ordained bishop.[58] This is a very clear statement of the teaching of the council about the Pope being a member of the College of Bishops. John Paul II explicitly noted this again in *Ut unum sint:*

> When the Catholic Church affirms that the office of the Bishop of Rome corresponds to the will of Christ, she does not separate this office from the mission entrusted to the whole body of Bishops, who are also "vicars and ambassadors of Christ." The Bishop of Rome is a member of the "College," and the Bishops are his brothers in the ministry. (§95)

Like the Church herself, the episcopate is a "pilgrim" episcopate, existing in the circumstances of history and place, bearing in itself the limitations of all humanity and walking in the certainties and obscurities of faith. There must, then, be some parameters for collegiality in the Church. There must be good order and coordination within the episcopate. The episcopate must not only manifest its collegiality; it must also manifest the other profound reality of the Church, communion:

> So that the episcopate itself, however, should be one and undivided, he [Christ] placed blessed Peter over the rest of

---

[57] See *Lumen Gentium* §20: "Therefore the synod [i.e., Vatican II] teaches that by divine institution the Bishops have succeeded to the place of the apostles as shepherds of the Church . . . ."

[58] See The Canon Law Society of America, *The Code of Canon Law: A Text and Commentary*, ed. James A. Coriden, Thomas J. Green, Donald E. Heintschel (New York: Paulist Press, 1985), canon 332, p. 270.

the apostles, and in him he instituted a perpetual and visible principle and foundation for the unity of faith and communion. . . .

But the college or body of bishops has no authority unless it is simultaneously conceived of in terms of its head, the Roman Pontiff, Peter's successor. (*Lumen Gentium* §18)

During October 1963, the new draft of the document on the Church was discussed by the council. As the discussion progressed, the majority and the moderators grew uneasy due to the seeming lack of direction from the Doctrinal Commission. The moderators of the council determined that it was necessary to get an expression of the bishops on four propositions which would then serve as a guide to the Doctrinal Commission in further developing the text of the document as successive drafts were presented to the council. Two of the propositions dealt with collegiality. The first of these is as follows:

The Body or College of Bishops succeeds to the college of the apostles in its function of evangelizing, sanctifying and pastoring. And this Body, in union with its head, the Roman Pontiff, and never without its head . . . , enjoys full and sovereign power over the universal Church.

The second:

This power belongs to the College of Bishops, united to its head, by divine right.

When the vote was taken on October 30, 1963, there were 2,157 bishops voting. Of this number 1,808 voted yes on the first proposition and 1,717 yes on the second.[59]

Clearly the great body of the episcopal magisterium held the doctrine of collegiality and held that it was not simply a matter of ecclesiastical or juridical institution. This became the solemn teaching of the council in the final document on the Church publicly approved by the Pope on November 21,

---

[59] See Grootaers, *Primauté,* 29.

1964. And it is worthy of note that two future Popes were participants in the council, John Paul I and John Paul II.

The distinction is often made between affective and effective collegiality. Affective collegiality is understood to mean a certain positive, friendly attitude among bishops. Sometimes this expression is used to attenuate episcopal collegiality and reduce it to nothing more substantial than courtesy, charity, and friendliness. This does not square with the Latin original of the expression, *collegialis affectus,* as used in *Lumen Gentium* (§23). The Latin word *affectus* means not only the state of feeling, but implies some objective thing or reason on which that feeling is based: in this case, the reality of the College of Bishops as such.[60] Affective collegiality, then, is an accompaniment of and is rooted in a real and objective episcopal collegiality. It is not simply analogous to real collegiality. It is a property of real collegiality.

Collegiality is embedded in the two doctrinal realities of *communion* and *sacrament.* It is the nature of the Church as communion and the episcopal office as constituted by a sacrament that give rise to collegiality. Collegiality is an essential quality of the worldwide body of bishops.[61] Just as Church authority determines the conditions for the celebration of the sacraments but does not itself create the sacraments, so Church authority regulates the functioning of collegiality but does not itself create it. And inasmuch as collegiality is clearly a divinely intended aspect of the Church, it must not only be grudgingly tolerated, but must be promoted and enabled to function in the most effective way. In fact, both Vatican I and Vatican II teach that a major, positive role of the primacy is to defend and promote the role of the bishops.[62] The gifts of God must not be neglected or stifled. It is

---

[60] Lewis and Short, *Latin Dictionary,* s.v., *affectus,* p. 66.

[61] See Charles M. Murphy, "Collegiality: An Essay Toward Better Understanding," *Theological Studies* 48 (1985): 38–49.

[62] Vatican Council I, *Pastor Aeternus,* chap. 3, in *Decrees of the Ecumenical Councils,* ed. Tanner, 2:813–15; Vatican Council II, *Lumen Gentium* §27.

not a question of whether the Church embraces and believes in the primacy of the Pope and, at the same time, in the collegiality of the episcopate, but how these realities are to coexist in a beneficial way without doing injury to each other. It is the question of the *exercise* of the primacy and the *exercise* of collegiality.

In times past one spoke of schools of theological thought, for example, the Roman school, the Jesuit school, the Dominican school. While such "schools" are not now commonly spoken of, it is still legitimate, I think, to speak of a "curial" school of theology. The tendency of this school is definitely in the monarchical line. It is reflected, among other things, in the way synods are held without a true public debate on points at issue, in the reserve shown by Rome toward episcopal conferences and the tendency to limit their teaching authority and, with some frequency, to reject their decisions. And so now we turn to two manifestations of collegiality: episcopal conferences and the Synod of Bishops.

Episcopal Conferences

In 1985 an Extraordinary Synod of Bishops was convoked to mark the twentieth anniversary of the Second Vatican Council. On that occasion a resolution was approved asking for a further study of episcopal conferences and particularly of their teaching authority.[63] Pope John Paul II responded to this request through an apostolic letter *motu proprio On the Theological and Juridical Nature of Episcopal Conferences,* dated May 21, 1998.[64] Joseph Komonchak notes that this document appears to make the universal Church an abstraction that exists apart from the real, particular, or local Churches.[65] The focus on the universal Church, he says, leads

---

[63] See Joseph Komonchak, "On the Authority of Bishops' Conferences," *America,* September 12, 1998, pp. 7–10.

[64] Official translation published by *L'Osservatore Romano,* July 15, 1998.

[65] See Komonchak, "On the Authority," 9.

to a diminishment of intermediate forms of cooperation such as episcopal conferences. This appraisal is further borne out by the provision of the papal document that in order to be published as the authoritative teaching of the conference, doctrinal declarations must either have been unanimously approved by the members, or, if approved by two thirds of them, they must also receive the approval (*recognitio*) of the Holy See. As Komonchak points out, "So stringent a criterion . . . is greater than any required in any other instance of ecclesiastical governance or teaching on either the local or universal level."[66] Unanimity is not required at an ecumenical council nor in the official meetings of the Roman Congregations. Since unanimity is not likely to be achieved, this requirement in effect rules out a doctrinal role for an episcopal conference. It is sometimes said that faith is not determined by a majority, but in reality, by force of this requirement of unanimity, doctrine taught by a conference is being determined by a minority, which by resisting the majority controls the vote. This unanimity requirement also creates the impression that there is a conscious intention to diminish the importance of conferences because under this statute they would rarely if ever be able to propose a doctrinal teaching.

Negative policies of Rome toward episcopal conferences will without question have a dampening effect on hopes for Christian unity. One reason is that the more episcopal conferences are limited, the more centralization is strengthened. Fear of too strong a centralization is one of the besetting fears Orthodox and Protestant Christians have in regard to establishing full communion with Rome. Rome's clear and repeated signals of distrust for conferences and the policies aimed at limiting them are also injurious to unity within the Catholic Church, since such policies create the belief that it is not necessary to pay attention to the episcopate of the country, that it is not competent or trustworthy.

---

[66] Ibid., 10.

With this in mind, it is important now to look at the teaching of Vatican II on episcopal conferences. In the Constitution on the Church (*Lumen Gentium*), the council developed its teaching within a theological and historical perspective. At the theological level, it presents conferences as a manifestation of God's providence, which first moved the Church to the formation of the ancient patriarchates (§23) (which were collegial structures), and then states: "In like manner the episcopal bodies of today are in a position to render a manifold and fruitful assistance, so that this collegiate sense may be put into practical application" (§23).

The expression "in like manner" is intended to convey an analogy of proportionality: conferences are not in every respect like the patriarchates, but these two do have certain qualities in common. In a section of the document whose general context is collegiality and which likens the episcopal conferences to the patriarchates, logic would seem to require the conclusion that conferences also have some collegial character.[67]

The council decree on bishops also views the modern episcopal conference as an organic development of the synods and provincial and plenary councils of ancient times. Whatever distinctions must be made, Vatican II does see a real link between conferences and those ancient institutions that were certainly manifestations of collegiality.[68]

Touching on this topic, Avery Dulles has written:

> [D]ivine law does give the hierarchy the right and duty to establish the structures that are found helpful for the exer-

---

[67] It is significant that while the apostolic letter on conferences quotes from Vatican II documents of lesser stature, it does not quote the foundational statement on episcopal conferences in the Constitution on the Church (*Lumen Gentium* §23) and its analogy of modern conferences to the ancient patriarchates.

[68] See "Decree on the Pastoral Office of Bishops in the Church," §§36–38, in *Decrees of the Ecumenical Councils,* ed. Tanner, 2:936–37.

cise of their divinely given mission as individuals and in groups.[69]

Dulles mentions besides episcopal conferences other institutions that are not of the essence of the Church such as parishes, dioceses, and the Roman Curia, but notes: "[T]hey have real authority based on the divinely established order of the Church."[70] Evidence of divine providence, these structures, though contingent, are rooted in the Church's authority to devise means for fulfilling her mission and in this sense are "based on the divinely established order of the Church."

The Second Vatican Council, then, does not reflect the idea that there are only two divinely based expressions of the episcopal office, the relationship of the individual bishop to the Pope and the formal united and collegial action of the bishops of the world in an ecumenical council. In addition to these, there is the providential development of episcopal conferences, which are not mere administrative conveniences but a reflection of the communion of the local churches in a region or country and a manifestation of the diversity and catholicity of the Church.[71]

In 1964, Joseph Ratzinger, a theological expert at the council, wrote:

> One not infrequently hears the opinion that the bishops' conferences lack all theological basis and could therefore not act in a way that would oblige the individual bishop. The concept of collegiality, so it is said, could be applied only to the common action of the entire episcopate. Here again we have a case where a one-sided and un-historical systematization breaks down.

It is noteworthy that the then Professor Ratzinger states that this view is lacking in historical foundation and that it is distorted, incomplete, "one-sided."

---

[69] See Avery Dulles, S.J., "Bishops' Conference Documents: What Doctrinal Authority?" *Origins* 14, no. 32 (January 24, 1985): 530.

[70] Ibid.

[71] Tillard, *L'Eglise locale*, 472.

He then goes on to say:

> The *suprema potestas in universa ecclesia* . . . applies of
> course only to the college of bishops as a whole in union with
> the bishop of Rome. But is it always a question of *suprema*
> *potestas?* We should rather say that the concept of collegial-
> ity, besides the office of unity which pertains to the pope, sig-
> nifies an element of variety and adaptability that basically
> belongs to the structure of the Church, but may be activated
> in many different ways. The collegiality of bishops signifies
> that there should be in the Church (under and in the unity
> guaranteed by the primacy) an ordered plurality. The bish-
> ops' conferences, are, then, one of the possible forms of col-
> legiality that is here partially realized but with a view to the
> totality.[72]

Jerome Hamer, O.P., like Ratzinger a professor of theology
and a theological expert at the council, later an official of the
Congregation for the Doctrine of the Faith and a curial cardinal, wrote in a similar vein:

> [T]here are not two episcopal collegialities, a universal one
> and a regional one. There is only one—that of the entire epis-
> copate and the pope. The conference is a legitimate historical
> and practical expression of the collegiality which is of divine
> right.[73]

Notice that here, too, Professor Hamer refers to the historical grounding of collegiality.

It is important to cite the positions of these two distinguished theologians because both subsequently expressed a
drastically different point of view. For example, where
Ratzinger in 1964 had said, "The bishops' conferences are,
then, one of the possible forms of collegiality that is here par-
tially realized but with a view to the totality," in 1984 he said,
"We must not forget that the episcopal conferences have no

---

[72] Joseph Ratzinger, *The Pastoral Implications of Episcopal Collegial-*
ity, Concilium (Glen Rock, N.J.: Paulist Press, 1964), 39–67.

[73] J. Hamer, O.P., "Les conférences épiscopales, exercise de la collegialité," *Nouvelle revue théologique* 85 (1963): 969.

theological basis."[74] And Hamer affirmed in 1976 that truly collegial actions can be posed only by the whole college of bishops and that episcopal conferences engage in "collective" but not "collegial" actions.[75]

But what led them to make such a drastic change? One probable reason was that problems began to arise in various countries with the development of large staffs of experts in the central offices of episcopal conferences. At times issues brought before the bishops are so complicated and the documentation so great that it is thought that some bishops simply defer to the judgment of experts without fulfilling their own personal role as judges and witnesses of faith. There was also the complaint that the role of the individual bishop was being minimized by a powerful majority and in effect individual bishops were forced to accept the decisions of the conference, which was thus interfering with the role of the diocesan bishops. The fear also arose that the conferences were becoming a threat to papal authority, reminiscent of the council-versus-Pope controversy of the late Middle Ages. This fear exists particularly in regard to a conference such as that of the United States, which has so many resources and such access to the media. The whole world hears what happens in the United States, and other episcopal conferences take note of what the American bishops do. Hence the fear that the American Bishops' Conference could become a force in itself and even a counterforce to the policies of Rome.[76]

In any case, it is interesting that both the later Ratzinger and the later Hamer appear to base their changed and negative views on the works of two other authors: Henri de Lubac and Willy Onclin, a professor of canon law at Louvain. De

---

[74] Joseph Cardinal Ratzinger with Vittorio Messori, *The Ratzinger Report* (San Francisco: Ignatius Press, 1985), 59, 60.

[75] See Joseph A. Komonchak, "Episcopal Conferences Under Criticism," in *Episcopal Conferences,* ed. Thomas J. Reese, S.J. (Washington, D.C.: Georgetown University Press, 1989), 14, 15.

[76] See Tillard, *L'Eglise locale,* 477–79.

Lubac made the distinction between the collegial and the collective act and denied that episcopal conferences were truly "collegial." But the position of de Lubac found support only through a selective reading of Onclin. Onclin, in a paragraph not cited by de Lubac says quite explicitly:

> Local councils and episcopal conferences may therefore be considered the juridical expression of the bishops' responsibilities as members of the college of bishops and of their concern for all the Churches. As such they are a manifestation of episcopal collegiality.[77]

It is reasonable to conjecture that both Hamer and Ratzinger, hearing complaints against conferences in their curial positions, found the work of de Lubac supportive in formulating their revised and more negative position on conferences.

Acknowledging the problems raised by episcopal conferences, Joseph Komonchak rightly points out the very grave and seriously harmful results that occur when practical issues become confused with theological issues:

> This almost always has unfortunate effects. When the practical questions are invested with ultimate significance, with wild charges that it is the very nature of the church which is at stake, it becomes very difficult to address them in and for themselves. In turn ecclesiology runs the danger of being degraded into an ideology, a defense of personal or group biases. Neither side in the debate about episcopal conferences is exempt from either danger.[78]

There is no doubt that complaints such as those mentioned do have some validity. Both the Orthodox and Anglican Churches have had similar concerns. With the Orthodox, the evolution of national and independent Churches has created problems. They are outside the structure of the patriar-

---

[77] Willy Onclin, "Collegiality and the Individual Bishop," in *Pastoral Reform in Church Government,* Concilium 8 (Glen Rock, N.J.: Paulist Press, 1965), 91.

[78] Komonchak, "Episcopal Converences," 22.

chates and can be injurious to unity and even to communion. With the Anglican Communion the same difficulties have arisen when individual Churches of the Communion think of themselves not simply as autonomous but as independent.[79] An example of independence was seen when the Episcopal Church in the United States unilaterally, and apart from the rest of the Anglican Communion, ordained women to the priesthood. Clearly there is also a reason for concern about episcopal conferences. There is a danger of nationalism and independence with consequent harm to catholic unity. Centrifugal forces do exist, and more than one observer has spoken about the congregationalism[80] very much alive in parishes which sometimes think of themselves as self-contained units detached from the diocese or from the rest of the Church catholic. Such a frame of mind can also develop in an episcopal conference.

But an ancient canonical principle is that "an abuse does not take away the use" (*abusus non tollit usum*). That is, simply because there are dangers to be avoided does not mean that a whole policy or structure should be eliminated or reduced to its minimum.

Is the answer to be found in diminishing the conferences? The answer should rather be sought in airing the problems, understanding their exact nature, and remedying them. A fact not to be overlooked in all this, however, is that some bishops who are negative about episcopal conferences do not take

---

[79] "Autonomous" in this context means that the Church in question is self-governing but in communion with the other Churches and working within the same doctrinal and canonical framework. Independent would mean that the Church in question is not only self-governing but has no accountability to the other Churches or to the center of the Communion. See above, p. 33 n. 41.

[80] I use "congregationalsim" here in the sense of isolationism. Parishes often think of themselves as all but independent units in a diocese. Certainly episcopal conferences can develop this kind of mentality. It is a danger not to be overlooked and at the same time a reason to promote true communion, which means not simply conformity but diversity as well.

part in the conference, never speak at its meetings and refuse to let their names be presented for conference office, but they make complaints about being intimidated by the majority or by the staff of the conference. For instance, a bishop now deceased told me that in twenty-one years as a bishop he had never spoken at a conference meeting.

Another issue in regard to episcopal conferences is whether they have authority to teach. Cardinal Ratzinger in 1985 stated, "No episcopal conference, as such, has a teaching mission."[81] Yet the 1983 Code of Canon Law expressly states: "bishops . . . gathered in episcopal conferences . . . are authentic doctors and teachers of faith" (canon 753). Reading the aggregate of the council teaching and the Code of Canon Law, it is difficult to see how one could reach the conclusion that episcopal conferences are not a true realization of episcopal collegiality and that they do not have a true teaching role. The apostolic letter on episcopal conferences affirms this teaching role but sets severe limits on its exercise. A striking example of an episcopal conference exercising its teaching role is the forthright doctrinal teaching of the German episcopate a century ago correcting the false impression that the Pope is an absolute sovereign and affirming the proper role of the bishops, a doctrinal teaching later confirmed and applauded by Pope Pius IX. The German bishops gave an authentic interpretation of a dogmatic definition, the correct meaning of the primacy of the Pope. This certainly is a very exalted form of doctrinal teaching by a national group of bishops.

The Synod of Bishops

The Synod of Bishops was intended to be another manifestation of episcopal collegiality. But it has been a great disap-

---

[81] Ratzinger and Messori, *Ratzinger Report,* 60.

pointment to many bishops from all parts of the world.[82] Patrick Granfield, who has specialized in the study of the papacy, maintains that the synods convened since the council have not in fact worked authoritatively with the Pope in major decision making and are in fact on the fringes of genuine Roman authority.[83] Today's synods seem distant from the ideal set forth in the council decree on bishops: "Acting on behalf of the whole catholic episcopate, it [the Synod] will show that all the bishops in hierarchical communion participate in the care of the whole church."[84]

The tendency since the council would appear to be to restrict the synod as much as possible. For instance, the synod is called by the Pope; its agenda is determined by the Pope; preliminary documents of episcopal conferences are not permitted to be shared with other conferences or made public but must be sent directly to Rome; the synod is held in Rome; prefects of the Roman Curia are members; the Pope, in addition to the Curial members of the synod, appoints an additional fifteen percent of the membership directly; the synod does not have a deliberative vote; its deliberations are secret, and its recommendations to the Pope are secret; the Pope writes and issues the final document after the synod has concluded and the bishops have returned home.

The procedures employed in the conduct of the synod also need to be reformed.[85] The synod opens with approximately two weeks of plenary sessions. During these sessions, each bishop may sign up to speak for eight minutes on a topic of his choice relating to the general subject of the synod. The bishops speak in the order in which they signed up with the

---

[82] See Patrick Granfield, *The Papacy in Transition* (New York: Doubleday, 1980), 32, 86.

[83] See ibid., 86.

[84] Decree on the Pastoral Office of Bishops in the Church §5, in *Decrees of the Ecumenical Councils*, ed. Tanner, 2:922.

[85] See Granfield, *Papacy*, 92–97.

result that each speech may have no necessary connection with what precedes or follows it. A bishop whose turn comes up several days into the session reads his prepared text without reference to all that has happened in the meantime. Often the speeches have been prepared before the speaker left his country for Rome. It would be difficult, in any case, for the synod members to read the other papers, since only summaries are printed in *L'Osservatore Romano,* and the full text of the speeches is not supposed to be made public. As these speeches continue one after another for two weeks in five languages with simultaneous translation, there is no debate or intervention. The assembly listens passively.[86]

It is only after two weeks that the bishops break into small groups according to language[87] and hold an interactive discussion. At the end of the two weeks of speeches and before the small groups begin to meet, a report is given to the plenary assembly on the speeches of the past two weeks.[88] An indication of the extent of curial intervention and control is the published story that the report on the speeches at the Asian Synod in the spring of 1998 was written on Friday, April 24, though the speeches did not end until Tuesday, April 28.[89] At the conclusion of the two weeks of speeches, the small-language groups begin to develop recommendations called "propositions" to go to the whole body for a vote and then to the Pope for his use in preparing a document for the whole Church on the topic of the synod. The Pope is free to use these propositions as he sees fit. There is no opportu-

---

[86] A source of considerable consternation among the bishops, especially the cardinals, at the recent synods was that attendance was taken, a sign that there was some concern about members not coming for these general sessions.

[87] Five languages are allowed in the synod: Latin, English, Spanish, Italian, and French. German may have been added recently.

[88] This report is called *relatio post disceptationem,* "report on the discussion."

[89] "Synod in Rome on Long Path to Enlightenment," *The Tablet,* May 9, 1998, p. 509.

nity for open debate about these recommendations in the full assembly of the synod. Usually the Pope prepares and publishes a document on the theme of the synod a year or so after its ending. Some Bishops stated that their proposed propositions were not represented at all in the final line-up of propositions.[90]

Among the questions that must be asked is why members of the Roman Curia should be members of the synods. Their membership only serves to enhance the idea that the Curia is not an instrumentality subordinate to the Pope and to the episcopate, but a coordinate body, a *tertium quid* between the Pope and the bishops. For example: in the recent Asian Synod a high curial official informed the bishops preparing the final propositions to be given to the Pope that they were not to use the word "subsidiarity."[91] This is an example of an ecclesiology according to which the Curia may determine what and how bishops may speak to the Pope even in a synod, an ecclesiology reminiscent of the maximalist position at Vatican I. Offensive not only to Catholic bishops, such behavior surely constitutes an obstacle for ecumenism.

Holding all the synods in Rome further underlines the aspect of curial influence and weakens the doctrinal truth about the full ecclesial character of the particular Churches. It has certain advantages, of course. In some political situations or in some cases of a very divided episcopate it may help to hold the synod in Rome, but these are exceptional cases. It is particularly dissonant when national or regional synods are held in Rome routinely.[92]

Even if the synod were not given a deliberative vote, it could still play an important role if it were conducted in such

---

[90] See Thomas C. Fox, "In Tug of War at Synod, Curia Gets the Last Word," *National Catholic Reporter,* May 29, 1998, p. 16.

[91] "Bishops Keep Up Push to be Asian," *The Tablet,* May 16, 1998, p. 640.

[92] It is, of course, sheer speculation but nevertheless an interesting question, whether China might have permitted participation of Chinese bishops in the Asian Synod if it had been held in Asia.

a way that the bishops were honestly and seriously consulted on issues about which the Pope intended to express his judgment or which the bishops thought to be of concern in the Church. An issue that comes immediately to mind is whether married men should be admitted as candidates for the priesthood. While this topic was addressed in a synod in 1971, the situation in many parts of the world is different now. Large numbers of dioceses everywhere are experiencing problems in providing sacramental and pastoral care for increasing numbers of people because there are no priests available.

In the interest of Christian unity, the Catholic Church must be willing to take some risks in the matter of a more functional collegiality. The parable of the talents could serve as a catalyst (Matt. 25:24–30). The one who was condemned in the parable was the one who had no vision and who was afraid to take any risks. To take a risk can imply a genuine evangelical prudence and authentic discernment. It is not the same as recklessness. John XXIII took a great risk when he convoked the council. John Paul II took a great risk when he invited honest reflection on why the papacy is and remains a great obstacle to Christian unity. All these are evangelical risks, taken in the name of the gospel and for the sake of the gospel. It is this kind of daring evangelical prudence which the urgent call for Christian unity demands.

Synods, if they were truly open and collegial events, could serve a very positive purpose. Synods, for example, could serve a purpose of preparing and refining the agenda for future ecumenical councils as well as dealing with more short-term or emergency issues in the Church. If this were the case, it would not require such a long time to hold a council. The likelihood is that truly open and collegial synods would enhance the moral authority of the Pope.

The official teaching of the Church proclaims that Christ intended the Petrine ministry to continue permanently in the Church and that bishops are successors to the apostles and those who exercised oversight in the early church. It declares that the episcopate needs a head for unity and coordination.

It maintains that the primate must have freedom to serve the unity of the Church and that he is not juridically bound by the agreement or consent of the episcopate, though he may be morally bound to seek their agreement and to listen to the episcopate. The Church teaches the sacramentality of the episcopate, that the Pope is a bishop by reason of the sacrament of Holy Orders as are all other bishops, and that the primacy cannot suppress, ignore, or diminish the authority and dignity of the episcopate. It teaches that both Pope and bishops are joined in the single College of Bishops, as both are joined in the one Mystery of the Church. The unfinished task—and an urgent one for Christian unity—is to articulate better, and in accord with the authentic tradition of the Church, how these realities function together without injury to either.[93]

Neither Catholic doctrine nor divine tradition indicates that the Pope should fulfill his mission by an elaborate centralization such as we have today. It is necessary to distinguish between the essential powers of the primacy and the circumstantial powers, between the habitual powers and the substitutional powers, between the fraternal powers and the paternal powers, between the usual powers and the emergency powers.[94] A distinguished Orthodox theologian, Stylianos Harkianakis, has pointed out that while the Orthodox find the language in which the primacy was formulated at the First Vatican Council unacceptable, they do not reject the idea of a primacy.[95] According to Harkianakis, the teaching on synodality and collegiality, so dear to the Orthodox, necessarily leads to the acceptance of one bishop as first among the others, who can express a decisive judgment in matters of concern to the whole Church while respecting the canonical structures of the episcopate and manifestly acting in conjunction with the bishops.

---

[93] See Buckley, *Papal Primacy,* 2.

[94] Ibid., 62–74.

[95] Ibid., 69.

There is a continuity between Pius IX's vindication of the teaching of the German bishops in the last century and the more developed teaching of Vatican II on the collegiality of the episcopate. The doctrine of collegiality is a context, a key for the interpretation of the primacy of the Pope. Doctrinally, Vatican II founded episcopal collegiality in the will of Christ, in the sacrament of Holy Orders, and in the nature of the Church as communion. In addition to the rare occurrence of ecumenical councils, Vatican II envisioned both synods and episcopal conferences as a manifestation of collegiality. It is not only the *doctrine* of Vatican II which is crucial to Christian unity; but in some sense, even more crucial is how collegiality functions in practice in episcopal conferences and synods.

CHAPTER 4

The Appointment of Bishops and Christian Unity

The process for the selection of bishops has enormous ecumenical importance. The Episcopal Church and Protestant Churches have considerable clerical and lay participation in the selection of bishops or church leaders. The Orthodox Churches select bishops through their metropolitan or patriarchal synods with the participation of priests and lay people. It is obvious that if the Catholic Church appears to have a closed process with a diminished, even inconsequential, participation of bishops, and little or no participation of priests and lay people, this will pose a grave obstacle to Christian unity. It will create fears that a possibile union with the Catholic Church will mean that they will simply have to accept bishops determined for them by a process in which they have very slight if any meaningful participation.

The selection of bishops is also a matter of growing concern within the Catholic Church itself. It is reported, for example, that Cardinal König, at the time archbishop of Vienna, was not consulted about the appointment of his successor in 1986. Subsequently it was reported that the religious superiors of his successor, a Benedictine monk, were not consulted, and that the successor was ordered not to inform these superiors of his appointment.[1] This mode of action has been repeated in various countries including the United States, where both diocesan and religious priests have

---

[1] Paul Zulehner, "The Austrian Test-bed," *The Tablet*, January 31, 1998, pp. 134–35.

been appointed to the episcopate without consultation with their bishop or religious superior. In one ecclesiastical province in which a bishop was to be appointed, only a few of the bishops in the province were consulted. The senior suffragan bishop[2] was among several others in the province who were not consulted at all. This is an indication that the opinions of the bishops are not valued or taken seriously. It should be clear that if some attention is not given to this and other aspects of the process, it will remain a major obstacle to Christian unity and increasingly a cause of unrest in the Catholic Church.[3]

It will be helpful to take a look at how bishops have been appointed in the Catholic Church during the past four hundred years (beginning with the Council of Trent) and also to see how other Churches select their leaders.

Appointment of Bishops in the Council of Trent

Speaking at the Council of Trent (1545–1563) about the three methods of choosing bishops then in use—nomination by the king, election by the cathedral chapter, and papal appointment—the bishop of Segovia, Martin Perez de Ayala, stated that abuses had crept into all of these three ways of choosing bishops.[4] This is a warning that there is not likely to be any "guaranteed method by which bishops can be

---

[2] A suffragan bishop in Catholic usage is the bishop of a diocese in an ecclesiastical province. For instance, in northern California, San Francisco is the chief diocese in the metropolitan province and is called the archdiocese. San Jose is one of the suffragan dioceses in the archdiocesan province of San Francisco and consequently the bishop of San Jose is a suffragan bishop in the province of San Francisco. The word suffragan is thought to derive from the Latin word *suffragium,* which means support or vote.

[3] "Once Again a Bishop's Appointment Divides Local Church," *The Tablet,* October 11, 1997, p. 1308; "Priests Worried by Choice of Bishops," *The Tablet,* December 20/27, 1997, p. 1662.

[4] Robert Trisco, "The Debate on the Election of Bishops in the Council of Trent," *The Jurist* 34, no. 3/4 (1974): 257.

selected to the universal satisfaction of all the parties involved."[5] It is also a statement that even in a system of papal appointment of bishops, abuses can creep in, as the bishop of Segovia pointed out.

At the Council of Trent few bishops wanted to change the royal power of appointment. Few wanted to eliminate the Pope's role of confirming appointments. At the same time, there was no sentiment for extending the power of the Pope. Most, however, were opposed to the cathedral chapters. It was chiefly the French bishops who raised the issue of the appointment of bishops, probably because the king had reserved the whole matter to himself for forty-seven years.

Opposition to cathedral chapters at Trent was based on several reasons. In many places, members of chapters were sympathetic to Protestantism; some were living scandalous lives, engaging in simony and favoritism and being moved by jealousy. A Hungarian bishop described the situation this way:

> For we see in Germany canons of twelve, ten, and eight years of age imbued with vicious habits. And here I shall not omit . . . that the secular princes usually interfere in every way and seduce, bribe, and frighten the canons into electing the one whom the princes want.[6]

Having rejected cathedral chapters, the discussion turned to the election of bishops by the people, the clergy, and the bishops of the province. Those who favored this cited the ancient fourth- and fifth-century councils of Nicaea and Chalcedon.

The arguments for election were essentially two: first, that it was the practice of the ancient church, of the medieval church, and, according to some, of divine law; second, that such a process would remove the abuses connected with royal nominations and chapter election.

---

[5] See John Tracy Ellis, "The Selection of Bishops," *American Benedictine Review* 35, no. 2 (June 1984): 125.

[6] Trisco, "Debate," 277.

Those opposing election denied any divine-law foundation for the practice and held that interfering with the royal
prerogatives would have negative consequences at a time
when the Church needed the support of Catholic princes for
protection against the growth of Protestantism. Since the
people could not be depended on to preserve orthodoxy, they
should not be involved in the selection of bishops. The
fathers of the Council of Trent did not have a high estima-
tion of the lay faithful: "[T]he conduct of men is changing
for the worse day by day so that today hardly any election
can be carried out calmly with the votes of the people."[7] Perhaps a more significant reason introduced against participation by the people was raised by an Italian archbishop,
Giovanni Battista Castagna. He pointed out the difficulties
that would arise if groups of people began to accuse and
oppose the candidate. In modern terms, this would be the
formation of blocs and interest groups. Castagna noted, "the
people, than who [sic] nothing is more fickle, is presumed to
be moved more by shouts, charm, favor, and sometimes
bribery than by prudence." Castagna brought up the example of the Council of Sardica in the year 343, which not only
did not accept the popular election of a certain bishop, but
even deprived him of "lay communion!"[8]

More tellingly, historian Robert Trisco notes:

> [I]t is easy to suspect that those who were opposed to cleri-
> cal or popular participation in the choosing of bishops were
> moved more by selfish, personal interests than by the concern
> for the welfare of the Church that they professed publicly.
> Many of them must have admitted to themselves that they
> would never have become bishops if the clergy and laity had
> any voice in the matter, and some may have dreaded facing
> the consequences when they returned home if they flouted
> their sovereigns' will at Trent.[9]

---

[7] Ibid., 283.
[8] Ibid., 284.
[9] Ibid., 290.

Trisco admits that this is speculation, since little is known about the personalities of the speakers. But it is speculation that has the ring of plausibility to it.

Since most of the bishops involved in the discussion were nobles, they would have had a negative view of the laity and of the general body of the clergy. At a tumultuous time of doctrinal conflict, it was understandable that they did not want to expand the forces involved in the selection of bishops. But a very important reason for opposition to election at the Council of Trent was that the elective process was not familiar to the clergy or laity of the time even in their civil life. Hence, there was no popular desire on the part of the clergy or the people at the time for election, and the bishops were not of a mind to try something untested and risky at a time of great upheaval. [10]

When the lengthy discussion was finally concluded at Trent, the status quo had changed little. Trisco sums it up:

> The result of the long deliberations was certainly in harmony with the general trend of the times. It was an age of developing absolutism. . . . The proposal to restore elections was contrary to the Zeitgeist.[11]

Between Trent and Pius IX

While no significant change was made in the method of the appointment of bishops at Trent, it is important to point out that in the intervening three hundred years until Pius IX (1846–1878) only a handful of bishops outside the Papal States were directly appointed by the Pope and very few cathedral chapters retained the right of election. Most of the bishops were appointed by kings and civil rulers.[12] Even so, there was provision for confirmation of election by the Pope.

---

[10] Ibid., 290.

[11] Ibid., 289 (*Zeitgeist* means "the spirit of the times").

[12] See Garrett Sweeney, "The 'Wound in the Right Foot': Unhealed?" in *Bishops and Writers,* ed. Adrian Hastings (Wheathamstead, Hertfordshire: Anthony Clarke Books, 1977), 207.

When Pope Leo XII died in 1829, there were 646 diocesan bishops of the Latin Churches.[13] Of these, 555 were appointed by the state; 67 were appointed by cathedral chapters or an equivalent. The direct appointment of bishops by the Pope, apart from the Papal States, was confined to twenty-four dioceses. These were in the Russian territories, Greece, and Albania, where there were few Catholics and the political situation was precarious and destabilizing. Garrett Sweeney observes: "It would evidently have been impossible at that date to say that 'the Roman Pontiff nominates Bishops without restriction.'"[14] It cannot be said, in light of this, that appointment of all bishops by the Pope is a necessary aspect of papal primacy, especially since universal direct papal appointment only begins after 1829.[15]

In roughly the last one hundred and fifty years, the situation has changed greatly. Writing in 1975, Sweeney noted: "Of some two thousand Residential Bishops now in the Latin Church, fewer than two hundred are subject to State appointment and fewer than twenty are elected by cathedral chapters."[16] The balance, some eighteen hundred bishops, are direct Vatican appointments.

The long-standing theology concerning the Church since patristic times would support the position that normally bishops should be chosen through a process that gives a major role to the local Church. I emphasize that it is not a

---

[13] This expression ("the Latin Church") refers to those Churches in communion with Rome which observe the liturgical practices of the Western Church as opposed to the Eastern Churches. They are called "Latin" because for more than a thousand years these Western Churches used the Latin language in the liturgy.

[14] Sweeney, "Wound," 218–19.

[15] Ibid., 231. Sweeney points out that in view of these facts, there is no history earlier than the nineteenth century behind canon 329 of the 1917 Code of Canon Law ("The Roman Pontiff freely appoints Bishops"), and consequently behind canon 377 of the 1983 Code.

[16] Sweeney, "Wound," 207.

question of denying the Pope's authority to reserve the selection of bishops to himself. It is making this the normal policy that is the problem for many. It was only after the middle of the nineteenth century that Rome showed any signs of a policy of appointing all bishops.[17] This is very recent, set against the background of two thousand years of history.

Four hundred years have elapsed since the Council of Trent dismissed election of bishops. Most people now are accustomed to elections in civil life. Thus, the *Zeitgeist* today is in concert with the doctrine about the Church as communion, with the teaching of the Church about public opinion, about the dignity of the laity and about their responsibility for and participation in the mission of the Church. Today, in many parts of the world the laity are more educated and literate than some of the priests and bishops and are already fulfilling roles of major responsibility in the Church. Historically laity and clergy have participated in the election of bishops, and there is an ancient canonical principle that "[w]hat concerns all should be discussed and approved by all."[18] Yves Congar shows how the participation of the whole Church in the election of its priests and bishops is an apostolic tradition.[19] There is every indication that in our times, in many ways so distant from those of Trent, there is a desire and a need to make the selection of bishops a more ecclesial event.

---

[17] Ibid., 211. Pope Benedict XIV in a letter of October 20, 1756, dealt at length with the Pope's right to name and to ordain bishops. But this was not a universal practice, as the facts indicate. See *Benedictus XIV, ep. In Postremo, 20 Oct. 1756* in *Fontes Iuris Canonici* (Vatican City: Typis Polyglottis Vaticanis, 1923), 538–49.

[18] Yves Congar, "Quod Omnes Tangit, Ab Omnibus Tractari et Approbari Debet," in *Revue historique de droit français et étranger* 35 (1958): 210–59.

[19] Ibid., 224–25.

Appointment of Bishops in the Eastern Churches

The procedures of the Eastern Churches in communion with Rome differ according to circumstances. Some of the Churches are within the territory of the patriarchate. For instance, Maronite Churches in Lebanon are in the territory of the Maronite Patriarchate. But other Churches are outside the territory, such as Maronite Churches in the United States.

The Code of Canons for the Eastern Churches stipulates that inside the patriarchal territory the members of the Permanent Synod propose candidates, about whom they may gather information by discreet inquiry among priests and prudent lay persons. This information is sent to the Patriarch, who may add his own observations, and then the entire list with accompanying information is sent to all the members of the Permanent Synod. After discussion and vote by the synod, a list of suitable candidates is prepared and sent to the Pope to obtain his assent. If eventually one of the priests on the approved list is chosen, the Patriarch informs him and the appointment is announced.

There are anomalies for the Eastern Churches in communion with Rome. Patriarchs of these Churches, unlike Orthodox Patriarchs, do not have jurisdiction over their communicants outside the patriarchal territory. Thus, if the election of a bishop takes place outside the patriarchal territory, for instance, in the United States, the bishops are appointed by the Pope.[20] That the Pope retains jurisdiction over Latin Catholics who live in the Eastern patriarchal territories, while the Patriarchs do not retain jurisdiction over Eastern Catholics in Latin territories, is a source of unrest and an ecumenical problem.

In the Orthodox Churches[21] which follow the Byzantine

---

[20] *Code of Canons of the Eastern Churches,* Latin-English Edition (Washington, D.C.: Canon Law Society of America, 1990), canons 181–89.

[21] The Orthodox Churches are understood as those Eastern Churches which accepted the decrees of the seven ecumenical councils of the first

tradition, a national assembly of the clergy and laity is held on a regular basis. When there is question of the nomination of a bishop, the assembly votes on three names, which are then submitted to the Metropolitan Archbishop and his Synod of Bishops or to the Patriarch and his Synod according to the status of the Church. The Metropolitan, or the Patriarch, and his Synod can choose any one of the three candidates, or they can send the list back and ask for a new list from the assembly. The highest ranking bishop—Metropolitan or Patriarch—is selected by the Synod of Bishops itself from among their own number.

This procedure too has its critics. In the Greek Archdiocese of North and South America, for instance, there has been some complaint over the almost exclusive appointment of native-born Greek bishops. Some Greek Orthodox feel that the Patriarch of Constantinople ignores the wishes and recommendations of bishops, clergy, and people in the appointment of bishops. In the last several years, the Patriarch named an American-born Archbishop for the United States, Archbishop Spyridon. The Archbishop had spent most of his life in Greece and Italy and has been bitterly criticized, even by other Orthodox Metropolitans themselves, for being too authoritarian, in other words, for not relying sufficiently on the synodal-collegial practices of the church.[22]

Appointment of Bishops
in the Anglican Communion

In the Anglican Church in England there has been some dissatisfaction with the appointment of bishops by the Crown. Before Queen Victoria (1837–1901), bishops were chosen by the Prime Minister and presented to the monarch for appoint-

---

millennium, but have not been in visible communion with the Church of Rome for centuries, perhaps as far back as the eleventh century.

[22] See "Greek Orthodox Leader in U.S. Faces Calls for His Removal," *New York Times,* February 21, 1999, p. 23.

ment without consultation with the Archbishop of Canterbury. Appointments were usually made on the basis of "national interest," a code for political reasons. Queen Victoria, however, insisted that the Archbishop of Canterbury be consulted. As time passed, a civil servant, the Patronage Secretary, began to do all the groundwork before the Prime Minister made any appointment, and the Archbishops of Canterbury and York were both consulted. Some Prime Ministers knew more about church affairs and clergymen than others, and some took more personal interest in such matters than others. In time there developed a private team of secretaries and advisors to assist the Prime Minister.[23]

Dissatisfaction over appointments of deans and bishops led the government to set up a commission to study the problem. In 1964 the commission presented its recommendations, called the Howick Report, proposing that each diocese set up a committee comprised of clergy and laity, whose function would be to make recommendations about what the diocese needed. The committee, however, would not propose names. This recommendation was implemented. This in turn led the Archbishops of Canterbury and York to designate their own advisors and not rest content with information supplied them by the Prime Minister's secretary.

Notwithstanding these developments, difficulties arose. The Patronage Secretary had other responsibilities besides the nomination of bishops and became overworked, with the result that appointments were slowed down. After he became Archbishop of Canterbury, Archbishop Ramsey also came to believe that the diocesan committees had too great an influence. It was his view that they focused too narrowly on the needs of their own diocese and did not give sufficient thought to choosing bishops who would also contribute to

---

[23] See Owen Chadwick, *Michael Ramsey, A Life* (Oxford: Clarendon Press, 1990), 71ff. The appointment of Archbishop Ramsey to Durham in 1952 was the first time in England that clergy and people were also consulted in the appointment of a bishop.

leadership of the Church at the national level. After Archbishop Ramsey's retirement, a modified system that reduced the part of the Prime Minister took effect. But this also had its drawbacks. Ramsey commented, "They don't get any better bishops and it takes them much longer to get them."[24]

The Anglican Church existed in the United States before the American Revolution but there were no resident bishops in the Colonies. After the Revolution, there were divisions among Anglicans between loyalists to the Crown and those who accepted the new nation. A difficulty in having a priest in the new nation ordained a bishop of the Anglican Church was that a requirement of ordination was that the bishop would have to make an oath to the Crown. Thus developed an autonomous Episcopal Church in the United States omitting reference to the British Crown. Consequent upon this development, bishops in the Episcopal Church are now elected in the diocesan general convention comprised of three groups: the laity, the clergy, and the bishop. A candidate must receive a majority vote in both the laity and the clergy. The bishop must then obtain majority approval from the body of bishops of the nation.

Among the advantages and disadvantages of this system are that reliance on the majority can tend to exclude minorities from election, for example, African-Americans or Hispanics. On the other hand, in fact, African-Americans have been elected to a major diocese, Washington, D.C. Jules Moreau, an Episcopalian theologian, observes:

> At a somewhat more profound level, nevertheless, the system does tend to produce bishops who are popular men and who might therefore be regarded as popular choices. . . . On the whole, the kind of bishop produced by this system is the popular and successful parish priest who has shown a capacity for leadership and a certain charism for getting groups and people to work together.[25]

---

[24] Chadwick, *Michael Ramsey,* 128–44.

[25] Jules L. Moreau, "Choosing Bishops in the Anglican Communion,"

The Episcopalian system has some negative features. Sometimes the convention will refuse to give approval. Sometimes there is a stalemate between the laity and the clergy, each holding out for its own candidate. Even so, defenders point out, this has not led to schism within the Church.

According to Moreau, "a greater threat is that of electioneering."[26] This involves private and even public campaigning with the attendant development of intense feelings for and against specific candidates. In some instances in the Episcopal Church in the United States this has left long-standing bitterness and deeply felt divisions in a diocese, although it has not led to open schism.

The Catholic, Orthodox, and Anglican-Episcopalian experience all reinforce the likelihood that no method devised for the appointment of bishops will prove completely satisfactory or yield results universally pleasing to everyone.

But the weight of Church doctrine, canonical principles, history, and the desire for Christian unity conspire to urge that we find a suitable way of opening the process of the selection of bishops to the participation of the whole Church while not exposing it to the defects that have been pointed out.

Toward a Change in the Appointment of Bishops in the Catholic Church

In 1972, the Vatican Secretary of State published norms for the selection of candidates for the episcopacy. While these norms call for some measure of consultation at the local level with priests, religious, and lay persons, they clearly retain the central role of the papal representative (nuncio or apostolic delegate)[27] with the ultimate decision resting with the Pope.

---

in *The Choosing of Bishops,* ed. William W. Bassett (Washington, D.C.: Canon Law Society of America, 1971), 76–81.

[26] Ibid., 83.

[27] There is a gradation of terminology for papal representatives. An

The papal representative is encouraged to hear various voices at the local level, to consult the bishops of the area and the president of the national episcopal conference. But it is the papal representative who draws up the list of names that is sent to Rome, and it is the Pope who makes the decision and is free to choose someone who does not appear on the list at all.

In recent years, even the modicum of consultation recommended in this document has largely disappeared. Sometimes there has been no consultation whatever with the local clergy. Bishops of the region are usually consulted. But it is not uncommon that only selected bishops are consulted, not all the bishops of the province or region. An important factor is that, so far as I can determine, no one, not even the president of the episcopal conference ever knows what names are on the list that the papal representative finally sends to Rome.

It has been the custom for the papal representative to invite the comment of all the American cardinals when a diocese becomes vacant. Because this consultation is done under the strictures of papal secrecy, the cardinals cannot be expected to ask the metropolitan about a diocese before making their recommendations to the papal representative. This limitation takes on added significance in a country as large as the United States, when cardinals living in the eastern part of the country make recommendations about a diocese in California, some three thousand miles away. The provincial bishops, then, never know either what the papal representative is proposing to the pope or what the cardinals are proposing to the papal representative.

Following publication of the norms by Rome, the Canon Law Society of America developed some concrete proposals for a procedure for the selection of bishops which were pub-

---

apostolic delegate is a papal representative sent to a country that does not have diplomatic relations with the Holy See. A nuncio is one who is sent to a nation that does have diplomatic relations with the Holy See.

lished in 1973. Among other things, the American proposal calls for the creation of a diocesan committee of ten persons, clerical and lay, who would through consultation, surface names of candidates. The diocesan bishop would also develop his own list but would submit it to the diocesan committee. The bishops of the province would discuss candidates, but only those which come through the diocesan committee. The list of finally acceptable candidates would be sent to the president of the national conference, and he in turn, with a committee of the conference, would make observations or accept the list determined by the province and himself send it to Rome. Rome would agree to choose only from the list prepared in this way.

These proposals were not accepted.

There is an implied ecclesiology at work in the present central role of the papal representative making secondary and even superfluous at times the role of the local episcopate. It is the ecclesiology of a monarchical, sovereign papacy above and apart from the episcopate. It does not reflect the ecclesiology of Vatican II, which is the traditional, patristic ecclesiology, an ecclesiology of the Church as communion, and of the Catholic Church being fully realized in the local Church in communion with the Apostolic See of Rome.

In light of this ancient yet new ecclesiology of Vatican II,[28] the primary role in the selection of bishops would more appropriately lie with the bishops and their Churches in the region. Bearing in mind two things—that the bishop is a member of a universal College of Bishops and that the Churches are bound together in a universal communion— the selection of bishops cannot be exclusively the function of

---

[28] It should be noted that Vatican II explicitly reaffirmed the teaching of Vatican I on the primacy of the Pope. Consequently, the ecclesiolgy of the local Church and the doctrine of communion cannot be said to be in conflict with this primacy in any essential way.

the individual Church or region. Consequently, there must also be a role for the national conference and for the bishop of Rome, with whom all the Churches are in communion.

A well-informed papal representative will have a sense of the overall picture of the Church in a nation and in other parts of the world, especially if he has had a varied and extended experience in the diplomatic service. This can be a valuable and indispensable contribution to the discussion of the provincial bishops. He may also have important information about individual candidates, which he should share with the bishops of the region. The nuncio should be a voice in the meeting of the bishops for purposes of information and comment. But respecting the authentic ecclesiology of the Second Vatican Council, it would be more appropriate if he did not make the final determination of the *terna*[29] sent to Rome. The logic of this ecclesiology would indicate that Rome should give priority to the local episcopate, not to the nuncio. In cases where the papal representative may differ with the local episcopate, his reasons and viewpoint should candidly and without any reservations be made known to the local episcopate and the problem should be worked out between the local episcopate and Rome. The papal representative should hold a subordinate role in the process.

Gathering accurate information about candidates is a very important matter. How this would be done effectively in a process that shifted focus from the papal representative to the local episcopate would have to be worked out very carefully. As with other aspects of the appointment process, it would be very advantageous to examine procedures in the Orthodox and Anglican churches.

The president of the national conference, like the papal representative, should have a subordinate role to the local episcopate. He should have no power to add or remove

---

[29] *Terna* is a Latin word and in this context means a list of three names sent to the pope from which he chooses one to name as bishop.

names, only to make suggestions and comments to the local episcopate. The traditional ecclesiology recovered by Vatican II would indicate that the list of names chosen by the bishops should be sent to Rome directly by the archbishop of the metropolitan province indicating the concurrence of the president of the conference. Any discussion of the list should be between the bishops of the province and Rome. The practice of the papal representative sending his own list to Rome should be abandoned. If for some reason Rome could not agree with the list, it should be returned to the province for further consideration and emendation.

Traditional ecclesiology and the long history of the church show that not only the bishops should be involved. Priests and lay people of the local Churches should also be involved in the selection of bishops.[30] Possible drawbacks exist as experience has shown: blatant politicizing of the process, factions and blocs, intimidation and little respect for confidentiality, which is especially harmful when it is a question of personal information concerning candidates' qualifications.

These serious issues require responsible consideration. This could be done by a representative commission of the episcopal conference taking a serious look at the experience of the processes used in the Orthodox, Episcopal, and other Churches as well as at the study made by the Canon Law Society of America. An important aspect of such a task would be the serious consideration of practical means to reduce or eliminate the negative factors that have surfaced in the various forms of selection in use in other Churches. When such a study is mature it could be presented for discussion and debate on the part of the entire national confer-

---

[30] If we are rightly to admit unfortunate historical events involving the participation of clergy and people in the selection of bishops, we should not overlook the fact that such bishops as Ambrose and Augustine were chosen by that means and were both members of the Churches which they served as bishops.

ence. In light of the discussion specific norms could be devised, discussed, and voted on by the conference and finally approved by Rome. This, of course, implies a different attitude in Rome, one that embodies the principle of the centrality and priority of the local episcopate in the process and does not reject their proposals altogether or make changes in them without true and honest dialogue.

Some Important Drawbacks of the Present System of Appointment

Testimony from all over the world points to a widespread dissatisfaction with the present procedure for the appointment of bishops. This procedure as it is actually carried out has in some instances produced serious problems, as the international press has reported in the Diocese of Chur in Switzerland and Sankt Polten in Austria, to mention only two.[31] In the former case, after years of complaint by priests and people and even by the Swiss government, the long-overdue change was effected.

But even if we were to say for the sake of argument that the present process has produced only the finest and most effective bishops, there is still something lacking. It is not a process involving the Church, and it even to some extent excludes the bishops. The present policy is injurious to the hope of Christian unity. This is so both because it weakens unity within the Catholic Church and because it is taken as a signal that the rich teaching of Vatican II about the local church is not fully operative or implemented in the Catholic Church.

One of the very damaging results of the present system of

---

[31] In these cases, the bishop appointed was not able to work harmoniously with the clergy and people of the diocese. In both cases there resulted widespread unrest in other parts of the country as well. In the case of Switzerland, after many attempts to reduce the problem by various means, the bishop was finally moved elsewhere. As of this writing the problem in Austria is unresolved.

appointments is the long delay in filling vacant dioceses. In the United States dioceses have stood without a bishop for over a year. This is extremely burdensome for everyone, especially in the modern world where contracts must be signed, where there are sometimes scandals of great notoriety requiring decisive action and leadership, in a world where priests are subject to greater and greater stress from declining numbers, increasing demands, and sometimes remorseless criticism, and need the coordination, encouragement, and leadership of a bishop, in a world where local and sometimes state legislation requires public response and leadership from a bishop—all these things make the lengthy vacancy of dioceses harmful to the Church and harmful to the mission of the Church. A still deeper problem in a lengthy vacancy is the theological dimension that the local church remains incomplete without its bishop as the sacramental sign of unity and communion.

Another defect of the present procedure is that there is strong emphasis on choosing candidates who can be trusted to be safe. It goes without question that one who is to be a bishop, a guardian and witness of the apostolic faith, must be truly orthodox and, like every other believer, must hold to the *regula fidei*,[32] guard the deposit (1 Tim. 6:20), and be prepared to die for the faith. But the problem is that "orthodoxy" can be confused with integralism.[33] Integralism may be described as a kind of narrowness and intolerance, raising private opinions and viewpoints to the level of dogma. Cardinal Newman finds an example of this mind-set in W. G. Ward, to whom he writes:

---

[32] This Latin expression meaning "rule of faith" comes down from earliest times and refers to the norm of orthodoxy found in the faith held by the universal Church.

[33] The French word is *intégrism*. Some writers in English use this French form. I have chosen the English form "integralism." For more on this topic, see Yves Congar, *Vraie et Fausse Reforme dans l'Eglise* (Paris: Editions du Cerf, 1950), 604–22.

> Pardon me if I say that you are making a Church within a Church as the Novatians of old did within the Catholic pale ... so you are doing your best to make a party in the Catholic Church, and in St. Paul's words are dividing Christ by exalting your opinions into dogmas.[34]

It should be possible to find candidates who are not only orthodox in the true sense but who are also endowed with critical judgment, imagination, and who are open to new ideas. Fidelity to the mission of the Church requires candidates who can listen, listen to the world, listen to the people, and who have the spiritual discernment and critical judgment to endorse what is good, reject what is evil, and not stifle the Spirit.

A significant problem ecclesiologically, pastorally, and ecumenically is the transfer of bishops to other larger and more important sees. From a doctrinal perspective the relationship of a bishop to his Church is not simply a functional relationship. It cannot be contained in the word "jurisdiction" or explained simply by his power to ordain ministers to the diaconal or presbyteral office in the Church. From very early times there has been a close bond between the bishop and his Church, even a nuptial understanding of this relationship to his Church. Canon 15 of the Council of Nicaea forbade the transfer of bishops on the grounds that it was a cause of "great disturbance" and factions; the council decreed that, should a bishop move to another see, his relationship to that see should be totally annulled and he should return to the Church to which he originally belonged.[35] A fourth-century local council in Alexandria called a bishop

---

[34] Letter of John Henry Newman to W. G. Ward, May 9, 1867. The full text of the letter is found in *Letters and Diaries of John Henry Newman,* ed. Charles Stephen Dessain and Thomas Gornell, S.J. (New York: Oxford University Press, 1973), 23:216.

[35] See *Decrees of the Ecumenical Councils,* ed. Norman P. Tanner, S.J., 2 vols. (New York: Sheed & Ward; Washington, D.C.: Georgetown University Press, 1990), 1:13.

who had transferred from one see to another an adulterer
and a synod at Carthage ranked transfer of bishops with the
heretical practices of rebaptism and reordination.[36] St.
Gregory of Nazianzus was forced to resign as archbishop of
Constantinople because he had been ordained first as bishop
of Sasima. Pope Damasus was among those insisting on the
resignation and precisely in virtue of canon 15 of Nicaea.[37]
Throughout the first millennium, Rome so consistently held
to canon 15 of Nicaea that no one who had been bishop of
another see was ever elected Pope until Marinus I in 882.[38]
This sacred nuptial bond between the bishop and his Church
was not the only reason that led the Church of earlier centuries to proscribe the transfer of bishops. The Church saw
that transfers could be often motivated by ambition and the
will to power. The local Council of Sardica complained that
"[a]lmost no Bishop is found who will move from a large
city to a small one . . . whence it appears that they are
inflamed by the heat of avarice to serve ambition."[39]

Transfer was not absolutely prohibited but could be done
by the action of the synod as an exceptional response to a
particular need. But the fact that it was rare and in general
forbidden considerably modified ecclesiastical ambition,
which brings with it other evils.

The transfer of bishops, unfortunately, has become com-
monplace. Some dioceses have repeatedly experienced the
transfer of their bishop after only a few years.[40] The frequent

---

[36] See Michael J. Buckley, *Papal Primacy and the Episcopate* (New
York: Crossroad, 1998), 90–91.

[37] W. H. C. Frend, *The Early Church* (Philadelphia: Fortress Press,
1965), 174–76.

[38] Buckley, *Papal Primacy,* 93.

[39] Ibid., 91–92.

[40] All the archbishops of San Francisco since 1932 have been transferred from other dioceses. Of these, the longest in his previous diocese
was nine years. In 1998, of the twelve diocesan bishops in California, six
had been bishops of other dioceses: two were thirteen years in the first diocese, one nine years, one six, one five, and one four.

transfer of bishops, in addition to feeding ambition, has doctrinal ramifications as well. It erodes the doctrinal understanding of the nature of the episcopal office, reducing it to an administrative function. It is demoralizing to the priests and religious and lay persons active in the Church, giving them the sense that their local Church has little importance. Priests cannot believe that the bishop has a genuine brotherly and pastoral concern for them if they believe he thinks his talents should be recognized by a "promotion" to another see. Since each bishop has his own approach and way of doing things, frequent changes cause confusion. In addition, transfers submit the Church, in some instances, to frequently repeated and lengthy vacancies. This is inimical to the pastoral good of the people. The issue of transfer, then, is one which for the sake of Christian unity merits much consideration.[41]

Catholic doctrine concerning the bishop in the Church also invites further consideration of the proliferation of auxiliary bishops. The ecclesiology of the Church is built around the single bishop as the visible principle of unity and communion in the local Church. The multiplication of bishops in a single Church is to some degree in conflict with this ecclesiology and with the provisions of the Council of Nicaea, notwithstanding the fact that even where there are auxiliary bishops, there is still juridically only one diocesan bishop. Important reasons for naming auxiliary bishops today are to assist with administrative responsibilities and confirmation. Fortunately the new Code of Canon Law reflects the mind of the Vatican II on this point by making it possible for the bishop to delegate priests for administrative responsibilities and for confirmation. Some object to the latter saying that the bishop is the ordinary minister of the sacrament of con-

---

[41] This is an affirmation of the traditional Catholic doctrine about the role of the bishop. It does not deal with the case of problem dioceses where the bishop does not relate to the priests or has other problems. This kind of issue needs to be provided for, but it does not nullify the general principle against transfer as a routine practice.

firmation. Vatican II considered this point and saw that this terminology could be taken as a criticism of the practice of the Eastern Churches, where priests regularly confirm, and that it did not reflect traditional Catholic doctrine. Consequently, the council abandoned the terminology of ordinary minister of the sacrament of confirmation and described the bishop as the "original minister" (*Lumen Gentium* §26).[42] There is therefore no reason in tradition or doctrine why priests should not be delegated to confirm, eliminating another reason for naming auxiliary bishops.[43]

A similar serious problem exists in the Orthodox Churches. The Council of Nicaea laid down the principle that there should be only one bishop in each city.[44] Hence, the multiplication of bishops of Eastern Churches, even those in communion with one another, is, in light of the decrees of Nicaea at least, an uncanonical arrangement. In San Francisco, for example, there are at least four Orthodox Bishops. In light of this the Patriarch of Constantinople in the early part of the twentieth century, addressing this problem as it existed in Central Europe, called the organization of separate Church hierarchies in the same place based on linguistic, ethnic, or cultural divisions the heresy of "ethnophyleticism."[45]

The Churches of the East and of the West are trying to deal with pastoral needs by the multiplication of bishops—

---

[42] See also Karl Rahner, in *Commentary on the Documents of Vatican II,* ed. Vorgrimler, 1:217.

[43] Some other reasons are given for the appointment of auxiliary bishops: the linguistic and ethnic diversity of a diocese, the value of having a certain solemnity in the liturgy that comes from the presence of a bishop, etc. These reasons need to be reconsidered in the light of the Church's ecclesiology and a deeper, more sacramental, and less juridical understanding of the episcopal office.

[44] See *Decrees of the Ecumenical Councils,* ed. Tanner, 1:9–10, canon 8.

[45] Memorandum addressed to the author by Steven A. Armstrong, S.J., April 28, 1998. "Ethnophyleticism" means a segregation of people according to nationality or language. Such practices, of course, do injury to commmunion, which means openness and reciprocity, not exclusivity and closed borders.

auxiliary bishops in the West and separate hierarchies in the case of the Eastern Churches. In both cases the pastoral principle is challenging the doctrinal-ecclesiological principle. Both the East and the West have a taxing problem in this regard. Both need to find a solution that does not overlook the tradition and the ecclesiology that each diocese should have only one bishop.

If the Church is to respond to the challenge raised by Pope John Paul II, if the exercise of the primacy is to be reconsidered in the light of the new situation, the serious issues involved in the appointment, transfer, and multiplication of bishops cannot be ignored. These are not only practical, administrative questions. They are doctrinal questions, and existing policies are rooted in a certain doctrinal stance, which badly needs to be examined.

CHAPTER 5

The Reform of the Papacy
and the College of Cardinals

There are two important structures that relate both to the collegiality of the episcopate and to the hope for Christian unity: the College of Cardinals and the Roman Curia. Both are so closely linked with the papacy that a reform of the papal office would necessarily mean a reform as well of the College of Cardinals and of the Roman Curia. The College of Cardinals will be treated in this chapter, the Roman Curia in the next.

At the present time, about three quarters of the cardinals are archbishops of major metropolitan sees throughout the world. The other one-fourth are the principal collaborators with the Pope in the exercise of his primatial office, serving as heads of the various departments of the Vatican. The modern College of Cardinals thus consists of bishops who have major responsibilities in the government of the church.

This distinguished body, which has a thousand-year history, has performed great service to the Popes and to the whole Church. Yet there are three problems related to the College of Cardinals: the cardinals as a special enclave within the College of Bishops; the cardinals and the Eastern Churches; and the cardinals and the election of the Pope.

Before taking up these three problems, it will be useful to have some idea of the history of the College of Cardinals.

The History and Development
of the College of Cardinals

The term "cardinal" seems to go back to the massive relocation of peoples from Eastern into Western Europe in the sixth

140

century. The term was originally used of bishops who were driven out of their dioceses by the invading tribes and whom Gregory I (590–604) appointed to other sees.[1] The understanding was that if their original see revived, they would go back to it. Originally, then, the title "cardinal" applied to a bishop who was serving a church other than the one for which he had originally been ordained. This is why, by the latter part of the eighth century, the bishops of the sees near Rome who presided by turns at the weekly liturgy in St. John Lateran were called cardinals: they were serving outside their own dioceses. The twenty-eight priests of the Roman churches, who also had the title "cardinal," were responsible for the liturgy in the four patriarchal basilicas: St. Peter, St. Paul, St. Mary Major, and St. Lawrence. Nineteen deacons also took part in these liturgies. These priests and deacons were called "cardinals" because they were serving in a church other than the one to which they were permanently assigned.[2]

With a different meaning, the title was widely used among the Germanic peoples to designate clergy who belonged to a church directly subject to a bishop[3] as distinguished from clergy who served private chapels and churches belonging to and under the control of nobles or wealthy individuals or families. In the eleventh century, several places in Germany as well as Compostela in Spain began to have "cardinal" clergy in the style of the Roman church, clergy who served a cathedral or shrine, for example, for which they had not originally been ordained. So up to a certain point the title was not

---

[1] The word "cardinal" comes from the Latin word *cardo,* which means "hinge." Hence the idea that these displaced bishops were attached, as a door to a hinge, to a church other than the one they were actually serving at the moment. See Charlton T. Lewis and Charles Short, *A Latin Dictionary* (New York: Oxford University Press, 1962), 291.

[2] See I. S. Robinson, *The Papacy, 1073–1198* (Cambridge: Cambridge University Press, 1990), 33–34.

[3] These priests depended on the bishop in accord with the image of the door depending on the hinge.

exclusively used in Rome.[4] It is interesting to note that even to the present day, two canons of the Anglican St. Paul's Cathedral in London have the title "cardinal."[5]

In the half century between 1050 and 1100, the preoccupations of the bishop of Rome began to extend more frequently beyond that locality and to take on wider proportions. More and more the Pope, in the effort to free the Church from secular control, exercised his claims, both doctrinally and in action, to a universal jurisdiction in the Church. Since then and during the past millennium, the international and universal aspect of the papacy has become predominant, while the Pope's actual role as the bishop of Rome has in practice diminished.

As a result of these developments, the liturgical responsibilities of the cardinals in the Roman basilicas diminished in importance. The emphasis changed from a local institution of the city of Rome into an institution international in scope— the College of Cardinals—a nomenclature that first appeared in the year 1150.[6]

After that time, in addition to Italians, bishops of major sees outside Italy were named cardinals. For a period of approximately four hundred years, until the Council of Trent, the cardinals resided in Rome delegating the care of their dioceses to vicars. Their presence in Rome, of course, facilitated the holding of consistories[7] three times a week. The law of Trent requiring bishops, including the cardinals, to reside in their dioceses and the formation of multiple departments in

---

[4] See *New Catholic Encyclopedia* (New York: McGraw-Hill, 1967), 3:104–5.

[5] *The Oxford Dictionary of the Christian Church,* ed. F. L. Cross and E. A. Livingstone (New York: Oxford University Press, 1997), 286, s.v. "cardinal."

[6] Robinson, *Papacy,* 41.

[7] See *Oxford Dictionary,* ed. Cross and Livingstone, 403, s.v. "consistory." Also Lewis and Short, *Latin Dictionary,* s.v. *consistorium,* p. 433.

the Curia, brought about the end of the consistory of cardinals as the primary body of advisors to the Pope.

From the middle of the twelfth century until the new Code of Canon Law promulgated in 1983, the College of Cardinals was described as a senate: "The Cardinals of the Holy Roman Church constitute a senate of the Roman Pontiff."[8] This terminology, borrowed from the structures and nomenclature of the Roman Empire, is also a sign of the juridicizing of the Church, so notable a feature of the Church since the Gregorian reform.[9]

Interestingly, the new Code of 1983 abandons the language of "senate" and refers to the cardinals as a "college." Thus, canon 349 states: "The Cardinals of the Holy Roman Church constitute a special College whose responsibility it is to provide for the election of the Roman Pontiff according to the norm of special law."[10]

The College of Cardinals: A College within a College

The first of the problems mentioned earlier in this chapter is that the College of Cardinals is a college within a college, in a sense making the rest of the College of Bishops a body of second rank.[11]

---

[8] *Codex Iuris Canonici* (Vatican City: Typis Polyglottis Vaticanis, 1917), canon 230.

[9] See Yves Congar, *L'Eglise de Saint Augustin à l'époque moderne* (Paris: Editions du Cerf, 1996), 107–12.

[10] *Code of Canon Law,* 1983 edition (Washington, D.C.: Canon Law Society of America, 1983).

[11] See also William Henn, O.F.M. Cap., *Historical-Theological Synthesis of the Relation between Primacy and Episcopacy in Il Primato del Successore di Pietro,* 227 and 239. In this Vatican lecture Henn states: ". . . the emergence of the College of Cardinals . . . was to some degree understood as expressing the collegial nature of the college of the apostles, with the effect of a loss of the sense of the collegial nature of the episcopacy."

Throughout its long history some kind of superiority of the College of Cardinals over the rest of the episcopate has been affirmed or assumed. Thus, St. Peter Damian, himself a cardinal, wrote in the middle of the eleventh century that the prerogatives of the cardinal bishops transcended the rights of all other bishops, including Patriarchs and Primates.[12] A document of this period, promoting the rights of the cardinal priests, states that they "possess the right of judging all Bishops throughout the Roman empire in all councils and synods."[13]

While this conception of the role of the cardinals is now recognized as grossly exaggerated, the spirit of these claims survives to some degree in the tendency to make the cardinals a unique and distinctive group within the episcopate. For example, the 1998 edition of the *Annuario Pontificio,* a sort of international directory of the Church, states that the cardinals are considered to be princes of the blood and for this reason have the title of "eminence."[14] Both the title "prince" and its specification here, "princes of the blood," are testimony to the appropriation of the secular, royal dimensions to this office. This certainly sets the cardinals apart from the rest of the episcopate.

That the idea of the cardinal as a prince is the popular conception of the cardinalatial office is reflected in a 1998 Sunday edition of the *New York Times* reporting the consistory at which cardinals were made. It carried a front-page photograph with the caption, "20 New Princes of the Church."[15] These exalted claims and titles appear in striking contrast to a gospel whose Lord fled when the crowds wanted to make him a king, who washed the feet of his disciples and who died in ignominy on the cross. We bishops also need to take these considerations much more to heart in light of the decrees of

---

[12] See Robinson, *Papacy,* 35.

[13] Ibid., 37.

[14] *Annuario Pontificio* (Vatican City: Libreria Editrice Vaticana, 1998), 1815.

[15] *New York Times,* February 22, 1998.

Vatican II. One thinks of the title "excellency," coats of arms, and other such things, which bespeak noble or royal prerogatives more than an apostolic witness.

There are other signs that the idea of the cardinals as a separate body within the episcopate still continues. An instance of this occurred recently in the United States. On March 24, 1999, the president of the episcopal conference made a strong statement about the hostilities in Kosovo in the name of the American bishops. Yet on March 31, 1999, the eight American cardinals as a separate body addressed letters to Presidents Clinton and Milosevic. An indication of the separateness of this act is that the cardinals' letters make reference to words spoken by the Pope at Palm Sunday Mass in Rome and to proposals made by the Vatican both to NATO and to the U.N. Security Council. But there is no reference in the cardinals' letters to the statement of the American bishops made by their president. This suggests that the voice of the bishops is not sufficient. It is also an indication that the cardinals see themselves as distinct and in some sense apart from the episcopal conference. If so, this is a serious problem. Like the past superiority of cardinals over the patriarchs, this too seems to be an example of the emphasis on the juridical over the sacramental.[16] The first problem, then, is the creation of a distinct body superior to and set apart from the rest of the College of Bishops, making the rest of the episcopate a body of secondary importance. The mention of rank has odious overtones. The Lord corrected his apostles when they were seeking the first places. What is at stake here, however, is not a first place of honor so much as dividing the episcopate into two classes. The doctrinal implications of this need examination.

---

[16] Congar, *L'Eglise de Saint Augustin,* 101n. 6. Here, it is true, Congar is referring to the cardinals assuming a superiority even over the patriarchs, as the triumph of the juridical. But it would seem to apply equally to the cardinals assuming some sort of superiority over the episcopal conference, being in some way distinct from it and above it.

The College of Cardinals
and the Eastern Catholic Churches

The second problem is the relationship of the College of Cardinals to the Eastern Catholic Churches. With Vatican II there came a new understanding of and sensitivity to the Eastern Catholic Churches. There was a desire to include representatives of these Churches both in the highest councils of the Pope and in the election of the Pope. Thus, some Eastern patriarchs were made cardinals. But recognizing the anomaly that it would be for patriarchs and bishops of the Eastern Churches made cardinals to be given the title of a Roman church or an Italian diocese near Rome, the new Code of 1983 provides that patriarchs of the Eastern Churches, if made cardinals, have the title of their patriarchal see and not a Roman church and that they belong to the ranks of the cardinal bishops.[17]

Even with these accommodations, making patriarchs cardinals is not a comfortable or satisfactory solution for the Orthodox or Eastern Catholics. To be made a cardinal is commonly thought in the Western Church to be the highest honor. But the dignity of patriarch is more ancient, and the Eastern Churches—Orthodox and Catholic—do not regard the cardinalate, a development of the second millennium in the local Church at Rome, as superior to that dignity.

The problem remains of how to incorporate Eastern patriarchs and bishops into the conclave that elects the Pope and how to include them in the advisory role held by the cardinals without diminishing in some way the dignity of the patriarchs or without linking them, even symbolically, to the local (Latin) church of Rome.[18] There has been resistance to an idea entertained by Paul VI of simply incorporating patri-

---

[17] *Code of Canon Law,* 1983, canon 350:1, 3.

[18] One objection raised by the Orthodox against communion with Rome is that the Eastern Churches which have communion with Rome have been "Latinized"; that is, they have taken on some aspects of the Western, or "Latin," Church.

archs as patriarchs into the conclave and not making them cardinals. This would seem to be the best solution and should be seriously reconsidered.

The Election of the Pope and the Ecumenical Perspective

In addition to the problems for the Eastern Churches, a third problem, created by the restriction of the papal election to the cardinals, is the wider ecumenical problem. Admittedly, this method of selection has produced outstanding Popes in the twentieth century, one a canonized saint and three others whose cause has been introduced.[19] In other words, election of the Pope by the cardinals is a system that has worked well. It should not be lightly changed, and, obviously, any change would have to be done with very great care so as to protect the election of the Pope from serious dangers not merely of interference from secular powers as in the past but also from other dangers.

A danger that comes to mind is raised by the election of the first non-Italian Pope in four hundred years, which has given rise to a discussion in the Church about the possibility of the next pope coming from the third world. The danger in this idea is that there could develop an expectation of a rotational papacy. This is the idea that the popes should be chosen from different continents in rotation—an African this time, an Asian after that, and so on. The rotational approach could be risky and dangerous because the expectation could become so entrenched that it might become practically impossible to choose the most qualified candidate because of the pressure to choose a candidate from a specific continent. This and other possible risks could be heightened by any change of the election process.

---

[19] Pius X (1903–1914) was canonized in 1954. The causes of Pius XII (1939–1958), John XXIII (1958–1963), and Paul VI (1963–1978) have been introduced.

Nevertheless, in light of the patristic and conciliar teaching on the Church as communion, restricting the election of the Pope to the College of Cardinals should at least be looked at not only with a view to including the patriarchs but also in view of the hope of unity with other Christians. In this connection the question should be asked, What bearing should the ecumenical factor have on the election process of the Pope? In the hoped-for event of the union of all Christians in communion with the see of Peter, how would it be possible to restrict the election of the Pope only to cardinals? Many Churches not now in communion with Rome are accustomed to participation by lay persons in the selection of bishops. How would the restriction of the papal election to cardinals be dealt with in a communion with these churches?

A significant issue ecclesiologically and ecumenically that is rarely raised in regard to the election of the Pope is this: What is the relationship of the papal role as bishop of Rome, to the papal role of primacy in the universal Church? Theologians have held that the universal primacy is rooted in the office of the bishop of Rome. This is reflected in the official Vatican Church directory,[20] where bishop of Rome is the first of the titles belonging to the Pope. The Pope himself uses this title nine times in the encyclical *Ut unum sint*. The office of bishop of Rome, then, is obviously something of primary importance to the primacy.

Yet despite this centrality of the office of bishop of Rome, it is the long-established practice that the Pope gives over most, if not all, of his responsibilities as bishop of Rome to a cardinal vicar, placing the focus on the primatial dimensions of his office. Very probably, in the election process no thought whatever is given by the cardinals to the diocese of Rome, the whole focus being on the universal claims of the primacy and which candidate could best fulfill them. In reality, then, the Pope's actual, pastoral role as bishop of Rome is almost nonexistent.

After the appropriation of the Papal States by the Italian

---

[20] *Annuario Pontificio* (1998), 27.

government in 1870, the Popes never left the Vatican until 1929 when an agreement called a *concordat* was reached between the Pope and the Italian government. Since then the Popes have made some efforts to exercise their office as bishop of Rome. No Pope has surpassed Pope John Paul II in this regard. He has visited parishes, met with pastors, ordained priests, and done other things associated with the role of the diocesan bishop. Even so, the universal claims of the papacy as they are now structured and exercised make it almost impossible for the Pope to fulfill in any but a symbolic way his office as bishop of Rome.

In addition to the delegation of a cardinal vicar, several other things show the *de facto* priority of the universal role of the Pope over his role as bishop of Rome. His installation as Pope, the inauguration of the papal ministry, takes place in St. Peter's Basilica, not in the cathedral of the diocese of Rome, St. John Lateran. It is true that sometime after his election the Pope goes to St. John Lateran for a liturgy. But this is secondary to the inauguration of the papal ministry in St. Peter's. Another sign of the *de facto* priority of the universal primacy over the office of bishop of Rome is that the liturgical calendar followed by the Pope is not that of the diocese of Rome but that of Vatican City. For example, in the Vatican, the Ascension of the Lord is celebrated on Thursday, while it is celebrated on Sunday in the diocese of Rome and in Italy. The same is true of Corpus Christi, a major feast in Rome and in all of Italy.

All this has come about over a period of many centuries. In view of the tremendous demands of the universal primacy as it is now exercised, it has a certain reasonableness to it. But that does not mean it should continue or, at least, that it should continue without serious examination. An examination of the *de facto* relationship of the primatial office and the role of bishop of Rome would have to confront the long-standing policy of centralization, which is one of the main factors preventing the Pope from devoting more attention to his role as bishop of Rome.

I raise the issue of the relationship of the primacy to the

office of bishop of Rome, because it is bound up with the election of the Pope. If more prominence is to be given to the Pope's foundational role as bishop of Rome, then in the election of the Pope some attention must be given to the claims of the diocese of Rome as such, and the candidate's qualities must be not only those required by the universal primacy but also the qualities required by one who is to be the bishop of this particular diocese.

These ecumenical and doctrinal questions merit careful and responsible discussion not only because of their inherent importance but because any change in the manner of election can have far-reaching effects on the life of the whole church. The three problems mentioned here—the college within a college, the cardinalate and the Eastern patriarchs, the cardinals, the ecumenical factor and the election of the Pope—show that some reform of the College of Cardinals needs to be considered.

Some Possibilities for the College of Cardinals

We have seen that the Popes have employed different structures to provide them counsel over the centuries: the Roman clergy, periodic synods, and the cardinals. The consistory of cardinals, in fact, took the place of the synod until the sixteenth century.[21] Pope John Paul II has revived this consultative function of the consistory. Between 1979 and 1994, he has held five extraordinary consistories, to which all the cardinals of the world were summoned.[22] The revival of the consultative consistory raises some questions.[23] How does the consistory relate to the international Synod of Bishops? Is this leading to a kind of bicameral structure? On what issues will each body be consulted? Which body has priority, the consis-

---

[21] Yves Congar, *Eglise et Papauté* (Paris: Editions du Cerf, 1994), 274.

[22] See Thomas J. Reese, S.J., *Inside the Vatican* (Cambridge, Mass.: Harvard University Press, 1996), 71.

[23] See ibid., 70.

tory or the synod? The relationship of these two bodies needs careful examination. Would it more clearly manifest the collegiality of the whole episcopate if the consultative function were reserved to the international synods? The synods would more directly relate to the episcopal conferences and have a wider membership than the consistory. A further positive development in the international synod would be a deliberative, not merely a consultative, vote. This much-desired change would manifest another doctrinal truth concerning the episcopate: that it is not only *sub Petro* but at the same time *cum Petro*. The episcopate *together with the Pope* has a responsibility for the whole Church.

The International Synod and the Election of the Pope

While history shows that other procedures for the election of the Pope were open to great abuse, it has also shown that the exclusive role of the cardinals in this process has also been open to abuse. In earlier centuries, for instance, there was the intervention of the noble families and kings, often relatives of the cardinal electors, in the process.[24] At times the cardinals themselves entered into pacts to follow certain policies if elected and even engaged in simony in order to be elected.[25] And so, while it is said that widening the electoral body could be open to abuses, it must be acknowledged that restricting it to the cardinals is not in and of itself a guarantee that there will be no abuses.

Certainly confining the election to 120 cardinals at the most creates a manageable electoral body. It also provides an important factor in that in a body of this size, which meets together from time to time in Rome and at other interna-

---

[24] Even as late as 1903 the Austrian emperor intervened in the conclave that elected Pope Pius X.

[25] Most seem to agree that these abuses have been absent from papal elections in this century and that the system of election by the cardinals has produced outstanding Popes.

tional gatherings, there is a greater possibility for the electors to form some judgment about the qualifications of various candidates. They know each other. These are weighty considerations.

Nevertheless, the College of Cardinals does not directly or structurally relate to the episcopal conferences. For this reason some provision for participation in the election by at least some of the presidents of conferences would seem to have merit. Likewise, since the Pope is bishop of Rome, some way should be devised to represent the Roman diocese in the election process. A way of doing this might be to consult the priests' council of the diocese of Rome about the particular qualities they see as needed in the next bishop.

Vatican II presented a strong and coherent doctrine about the role of lay persons in the Church. This doctrine has been greatly expanded and enriched by Pope John Paul II. In light of this, serious consideration should be given to how lay persons might have a part in the election of the Pope. Legitimate Catholic lay organizations in a country could be invited to express their view on the more important qualities they would like to see in the next Pope. This information could be coordinated and presented to the electors at the time of the election. The exclusion of lay persons from the process of the election of the Pope in the past was not due to a theological doctrine that lay persons could not have such a role. It was due, at a certain point in history, to an effort to wrest the electoral process from scheming and even simoniac noble families, from kings and from trendy, superficial, and sometimes violent forces of public opinion.

Theological understanding of the dignity of the lay person is much more developed today, and ecclesiology has recovered an understanding of the Church that goes beyond the papacy and the episcopate.[26] Whatever the problems involved,

---

[26] For instance, ecclesiology taught to future priests in seminaries before Vatican II was all but exclusively a study of the primacy and jurisdiction of the Pope and usually tinctured by the maximalist interpretation

careful consideration should be given to how lay persons could be included[27] in some meaningful way while at the same time finding ways to guard against the abuses especially associated with modern pressure groups and the tremendous power of the media. Obviously this is a matter of grave importance which requires careful study and true spiritual discernment.

Prudence and Evangelical Daring

The Gospels reveal the necessity of prudence when it presents the image of a man building a tower and sitting down beforehand to make sure he has the wherewithal to accomplish the task (Luke 14:28–30). But prudence is not the whole of the Gospel. It also cautions against excessive diffidence when it condemns the man who received the sum of money and buried it so that it would not be lost (Luke 19:20–24). Some steps must be taken which will constitute a calculated risk. Questions must be asked—are being asked—which may lead to answers not anticipated, answers that do not fit predetermined expectations, answers perhaps not enthusiastically welcomed at first, but which, because they are the providential answers, will bring rich fruit in due time. In this light, serious reflection on changes and reform of the College of Cardinals in light of the problems raised in this chapter has great importance for Christian unity as well for the effective funtioning of an authentic episcopal collegiality in the Church.

---

of Vatican I. There was also some study of the episcopate. See T. Zapelena, S.J., *De Ecclesia Christi,* 2 vols. (Rome: Gregorian University Press, 1946, 1954).

[27] I have debated about including an explicit reference to religious. I think they should be included. But, strictly speaking, religious who are not priests are included in the mention of the laity. On the other hand, today if one mentions religious one must also mention secular institutes, societies of apostolic life, and various other forms of consecrated life that do not call themselves "religious." To mention religious alone could be interpreted as excluding these others, and to mention them all by name could be exhausting for both the writer and the reader.

CHAPTER 6

The Reform of the Roman Curia

Anyone familiar with the Roman Curia knows that curial reform is needed not because of the lack of competence among its officials, or because of the lack of great, even heroic devotion on the part of many of its members, or because of the failure to update some of its structures and procedures. The need for reform is more basic. It lies in the failure to embrace adequately the implications of three truths: first, that the Church is not simply a monolithic structure with an omnicompetent central administration; second, that the Church, according to its own teaching and doctrine, is a communion of Churches, each of which has its place and its role to play in the life of the whole Church; third, that the bishops are not "mere papal functionaries with no personal responsibility,"[1] field managers who work only under instructions from central authority. This third truth, so compellingly affirmed by the German bishops in the nineteenth century, was forcefully approved by Pius IX at the time and again taught by Vatican II.[2]

The failure to embrace the consequences of these three truths leads the Curia to resist three things which, if not more fully implemented, will be a continuing stumbling block to Christian unity: collegiality, subsidiarity, and legitimate diver-

---

[1] F. Donald Logan, "The 1875 Statement of the German Bishops on Episcopal Powers," *The Jurist* 21 no. 3 (July 1961): 291.

[2] See chapter 3, pp. 78–81 above; see also *Lumen Gentium* §27 (see above, chapter 1 n. 6).

sity.[3] In order to have some perspective on the issue of the Roman Curia, it will be useful to consider its history.

The History of the Roman Curia

The New Testament bears witness that the apostles had helpers in carrying out their mission. Peter and Paul, for example, used secretaries (Rom. 16:22; 1 Pet. 5:12).[4] When controversy arose over allegations of discrimination in the allocation of food subsidies to the Hellenist widows in the community at Jerusalem, the apostles chose seven men whom they delegated to resolve the problem (Acts 6:1–6).[5] There are also co-workers in the apostolic ministry, among them Timothy, to whom two New Testament letters are addressed, and Phoebe, Prisca, Aquila, and others mentioned in the sixteenth chapter of Romans.

This kind of support for the apostolic ministry continued to develop, and by the fourth century notaries were a part of the papal service. The notaries wrote letters, kept records of correspondence, took minutes, and prepared the acts of important meetings such as local councils. Sometimes the popes sent them on diplomatic missions to councils in the East.[6]

At this same period, the priests and deacons of Rome were the Pope's chief advisors. After the liberation of the Church by Constantine in the early part of the fourth century, the Church for the first time could legally own property, and gifts

---

[3] This is understood in the context of chapters 1 and 3.

[4] A fuller development of this subject is found in Jerome Murphy-O'Connor, *Paul the Letter-Writer* (Collegeville, Minn.: Liturgical Press, 1995), 1–37.

[5] These seven men are not referred to as deacons. For more on this, see Richard J. Dillon, "Acts of the Apostles," in *The New Jerome Biblical Commentary*, ed. Raymond E. Brown, Joseph A. Fitzmyer, Roland E. Murphy (Englewood Cliffs, N.J.: Prentice Hall, 1990), 739–40.

[6] See Thomas J. Reese, S.J., *Inside the Vatican* (Cambridge, Mass.: Harvard University Press, 1996), 107.

of lands were given to the Roman Church. This led to the creation of management and fiscal offices surrounding the Pope. From the eighth century, the bishops of the dioceses near Rome joined the Roman clergy as advisors to the Pope.[7] These various services to the Pope gradually developed until the eleventh century, when the Pope's helpers were first called the Roman Curia.[8]

After the twelfth century, the consistory (the meeting of cardinals) held the primary role in advising the Pope, and the advisory role of the clergy of Rome and neighboring bishops diminished. The consistory met three times a week. Until the sixteenth century and the creation of multiple congregations in the Curia, the consistory was superior to the Curia as such.[9] In the thirteenth century, due to the growing centralization and juridicizing of the Church, tribunals were created for the purpose of hearing disputes and rendering decisions. These developed into the courts known as the Roman Rota and the Signatura, which continue today as part of the Curia. In 1542, Paul III created a "congregation" or group of designated cardinals within the College of Cardinals. This group was called by the imposing title "The Sacred Congregation of the Universal Inquisition."[10] Its purpose was to defend the Church against heresy.

But it was really Sixtus V, in the late sixteenth century, who established the Roman Curia with multiple congregations

---

[7] These neighboring bishops are often called "suburbicarian" bishops—the bishops of the suburbs we might say today. Besides the Roman clergy and neighboring bishops who were near at and for consultation with the Pope, more important matters were dealt with through Roman councils involving bishops from other parts of Italy.

[8] See Ignazio Gordon, "Curia: Historical Evolution," in *Sacramentum Mundi* (New York: Herder & Herder, 1968), 2:49–52.

[9] Klaus Mörsdorf, "Decree on the Bishops' Pastoral Office in the Church: History of the Decree," in *Commentary on the Documents of Vatican II*, ed. Herbert Vorgrimler (New York: Herder & Herder, 1968), 2:173.

[10] See *Annuario Pontificio* (1998), *Note Storiche*, p. 1834.

and tribunals along the lines of the present-day Curia. With this development, the consistory of cardinals lost its importance, as the Pope turned more to the heads of these curial offices for consultation and advice.[11] There was, then, an evolution in the advisory body surrounding the Pope: the clergy of Rome and neighboring bishops, the Roman councils, the consistory of cardinals, and, finally, the heads of the Roman Curia.

The modern Roman Curia is a large bureaucracy of some 1,740 persons. Thomas Reese comments that "[f]ew people either inside or outside the curia understand its complex structure, overlapping jurisdictions, and Byzantine procedures."[12] The structures of the Curia have been copied from secular governments such as the Roman senate, the Byzantine imperial court and the French chancery.[13] This must be kept in mind when we hear people today attack any "democratization" of the Church as contrary to its divine constitution.[14]

In the twentieth century, three Popes—Pius X, Paul VI, and John Paul II—have introduced changes into the Curia, but many believe that these changes do not constitute an adequate reform of the Curia.[15]

Calls for Reform

Cardinal Franz König, archbishop emeritus of Vienna, writing in March 1999, nearly thirty-five years after Vatican II, underlined the urgency of doing something about the extreme centralization characteristic of church government at the present time. The cardinal stated forthrightly, "In fact, however, *de facto* and not *de jure,* intentionally or unintentionally, the curial authorities working in conjunction with the Pope have

---

[11] See Gordon, "Curia," 49–50.

[12] Reese, *Inside the Vatican,* 109.

[13] Ibid., 138.

[14] One of the oldest and most democratic processes in the world is the election of the Pope by the College of Cardinals.

[15] Reese, *Inside the Vatican,* 280.

appropriated the tasks of the episcopal college. It is they who now carry out almost all of them."[16] Cardinal König referred to the need for greater subsidiarity and to the problem of the appointment of bishops without adequate participation of the local episcopate.

There are many examples of centralization great and small. Among them I might cite three. Under present provisions, an alcoholic priest, who cannot take even the modicum of wine used in the celebration of Mass, must apply directly to Rome for permission to use what is called *mustum*[17] as a substitute. The bishop, who knows the priest and the local situation, cannot give such permission. Another example is the laicization of priests. Laicization is now an accepted policy in the Church. Yet the diocesan bishop, or bishops of the province who know the priest and who know the pastoral situation of their area best, are not able to grant such a laicization. It must be granted by Rome.[18]

An example of involvement by the Curia in a matter of seemingly little consequence is the granting of honorary

---

[16] Cardinal Franz König, "My Vision for the Church of the Future," *The Tablet,* March 27, 1999, p. 434. Notice that the kind of centralization mentioned by Cardinal König involves the assumption of the role and prerogatives of the episcopate.

[17] *Mustum* is a form of grape juice in the very early stages of fermentation. St. Thomas holds that *mustum* is valid for use in the Eucharist, though it is to be used only for exceptional reasons (*Summa Theologiae,* III, q. 74, a. 5, ad 3).

[18] A problem regarding laicization exists at the present time. There are those priests who spontaneously ask to be laicized. This kind of case would seem to be best handled at the local level, not going beyond the episcopal conference at most. But there is also the case of a priest who has given grave public scandal and who may not petition for laicization but whom the bishop believes should be laicized for his own good and for the good of the Church. There is the possibility of bishops being arbitrary in this kind of case, and so there is a need to ensure that the rights of the priest in question are not overlooked. Thus there is need for some mechanism beyond the local bishop himself. But this does not mean that it has to be Rome. It could very well be a body set up at the regional or national level that would review such a case.

degrees. Several years ago a pontifical school granted me an honorary doctorate in theology. But before the degree could actually be conferred the action had to be approved by the Secretariat of State, the Congregation for Catholic Education, and the Congregation for the Doctrine of the Faith. While this triple approval is indeed an extraordinary endorsement, it seems quite out of proportion with the major concerns of those curial bodies as well as an injury to what communion of bishops with the Pope means. It would suggest that a bishop in communion with the Pope could be rejected as a candidate for an *honorary* degree yet would have the qualities necessary to be a teacher and witness of faith as a bishop. These are only a few examples of the extreme centralization that now exists.

The bishops of New Zealand, addressing the Pope at a meeting in Rome, made a point similar to that made by Cardinal König: "[W]ithin the household of the Catholic Church itself, Dicasteries[19] of the Holy See occasionally make norms which impinge on the ministry of bishops with little or no consultation of the episcopate as such. This seems inconsistent."[20]

The theme of the assumption of episcopal authority by the Curia appeared also in the Asian Synod (April–May 1998). Bishop John Cummins of Oakland, California, a participant in that synod, wrote: "Subsidiarity and inculturation were a constant theme."[21] They were a constant theme precisely because the bishops of Asia felt a lack of freedom to address the issues of their churches according to their own judgment as pastors. Bishop Cummins mentions some who addressed this theme: the Vietnamese bishops, the archbishop of Nagasaki, a Syro-Malabar bishop, the auxiliary bishop of Seoul,

---

[19] The word "dicastery" comes from the Greek word *dikastērion,* which means a court. It has come to mean an office or bureau. This word is in common use in Vatican parlance.

[20] Peter James Cullinane, "A Time to Speak Out," *The Tablet,* November 22, 1998, p. 1589.

[21] Letter of Bishop John Cummins to the author, September 4, 1998.

and bishops from the Philippines, Indonesia, and India. This concern was widespread among the Asian bishops. One example appears in a speech given at the synod by Bishop Francis Hadisumarta of Indonesia. Speaking of liturgical translations, he said, "Episcopal conferences have overseen liturgical translation and adaptation. At present all this vital work has to go to Rome for approval—to people who just do not speak or understand our language!"[22] Of episcopal conferences he said:

> Theology, spirituality, law and liturgy should be as diverse as our languages and cultures. In the future this should lead to a change in the relationship between the episcopal conference and the various Roman dicasteries. The Roman Curia would then become a clearing house for information, support, and encouragement rather than a universal decision maker.

Bishops in many other countries of the world, including the United States, Latin America, and Africa, share these three converging viewpoints from Europe, Oceania, and Asia. It is evident that some of the same problems that existed before Vatican II in regard to the Curia continue to exist more than three decades later. Rooted in centralization, these problems can be reduced to three general categories: the frequent overruling of the decisions of episcopal conferences, the appointment of bishops with little or no participation of the local episcopate, and the treatment of theologians. The most recent example of the latter is the questioning by the Congregation for the Doctrine of the Faith of the distinguished Jesuit theologian Father Jacques Dupuis. Evidence that there is something that needs attention in this procedure is the fact that Cardinal König, the bishops of India and the Jesuit provincials of India, and the former Dean of Theology at the Gregorian University have all either publicly questioned this intervention or publicly defended Father Dupuis. The fact

---

[22] Bishop Hadisumarta/Synod for Asia, "Enhanced Role for Bishops' Conferences," *Origins* 27, no. 46 (May 7, 1998): 773–74.

that all of these are respected leaders in the Church should be indicative of the need for serious revision of these policies and procedures.

Since there is dissatisfaction with the policies of the Curia among bishops in all parts of the world, there are obvious implications for Christian unity. Any movement toward communion with Rome will be dampened or deterred by the appearance of a Curia that takes away or seriously diminishes the legitimate role of local episcopates. This widespread dissatisfaction leads to the need to look at just what the attitude of the bishops at Vatican II was, and what their official decisions were concerning the reform of the Roman Curia.

Reform of the Curia at Vatican II

During the preparatory stages of Vatican II, there was a strong cry for decentralization and for a reform of the Roman Curia.[23] At that time (1959–1962) various reasons were given for the negative attitude of many bishops toward the Curia. For some, the Curia was a barrier between the episcopate and the Pope. Others regarded the Curia as high-handed and autocratic, superior to the bishops. Speaking of the attitude of many, even very conservative bishops at the time of Vatican II, the Belgian theologian Edward Schillebeeckx, a theological expert at the council, said, "Many bishops were less concerned with a renewal of theology than with breaking the power of the Curia, which considered itself above the bishops."[24]

---

[23] See Kevin Smyth, "Curia: Reform and Present Structure," in *Sacramentum Mundi*, 2:52. See also Reese, *Inside the Vatican*, 106. It is interesting to recall that Cardinal Morone, one of the papal legates at the Council of Trent, regarded the reform of the Curia as the most imporant of all the problems of reform at the council. This is indeed significant, given the very grave doctrinal and disciplinary issues dealt with at Trent. See Hubert Jedin, *Crisis and Closure of the Council of Trent*, Sheed & Ward Stagbooks (London/Melbourne: Sheed & Ward, 1967), 108.

[24] Edward Schillebeeckx, *Je suis un theologien heureux* (Paris: Editions

Aware of these strong feelings about the Curia among bishops at Vatican II,[25] Paul VI himself invited the council to discuss the issue.[26] The results of the council discussion of the reform of the Curia are found in the decree on the Bishops' Pastoral Office in the Church.[27] The decree calls for a reorganization of the Curia more in accord with the needs of the times and the diversity of places and rites in the Church. In other words, a reformed Curia should more manifestly take into account the great diversity in the Church, geographical, cultural, and historical, not only in its composition but more importantly in its policies and procedures. Specifically, Vatican II called for three things: (1) internationalization, (2) better communication and coordination among the departments of the Curia, and (3) participation by diocesan bishops and by lay persons.[28]

1. Internationalization

Since the end of Vatican II in 1965, there has been, in fact, a significant internationalization in the Curia. At least two-thirds of the heads of Vatican congregations come from countries other than Italy,[29] and there is a notable increase in the number of non-Italians on the staffs of the Congregations as well.

---

du Cerf, 1995), 46. See also Giuseppe Alberigo and Joseph Komonchak, *History of Vatican II,* vol. 2 (Maryknoll, N.Y.: Orbis Books; Leuven: Peeters, 1997), 214.

[25] See Smyth, "Curia: Reform and Present Structure," 52.

[26] Ibid.

[27] "Decree on the Pastoral Office of Bishops in the Church," §§9, 10, in *Decrees of the Ecumenical Councils,* ed. Norman P. Tanner, S.J., 2 vols. (New York: Sheed & Ward; Washington, D.C.: Georgetown University Press, 1990), 2:923–24.

[28] Ibid., §10.

[29] For more detailed information on the internationalization of the Curia, see Reese, *Inside the Vatican,* chapter 6, "Vatican Officials," pp. 140–72.

Internationalization was meant to bring people with different experiences and outlooks into the Curia and thereby create a broader vision in the Curia. The problem is that it easily happens that curial officials and staff lose their national identity, become Romanized, and lose real contact with their countries and with the pastoral realities of the churches from which they come.[30]

Nor does the way members of the Curia are chosen help create this broader vision the council had in mind. Names of candidates for the congregations or councils are surfaced by the head of the department and the Secretariat of State. There is usually no consultation with the episcopal conference of the country from which the candidate comes. They are often chosen not so much because they will bring a fresh outlook or approach as because they are in accord and in sympathy with the prevailing curial ethos and viewpoint. It is thus possible to have internationalization of membership without internationalization of mentality.[31]

2. Better Communication and Coordination among Departments of the Curia

Vatican II also called for better coordination among departments of the Curia. That this is still a problem is shown by

---

[30] Ibid., 142. See also Klaus Mörsdorf, "Decree on the Bishops' Pastoral Office in the Church," §10, in *Commentary on the Documents of Vatican II,* ed. Vorgrimler, 2:212. When the word "Romanized" is used, it is necessary to make distinctions. What is meant here is taking on the Curia's ways of thinking and of seeing things, of thinking of the Curia as the center and the rest of the Church as the periphery. Internationalization was conceived as a means of broadening this outlook. "Romanized" may be used in another and positive sense, meaning communion with the bishop of Rome and thus with all the other churches in the faith handed down by the apostles.

[31] Reese, *Inside the Vatican,* 142. See also p. 122: "The high percentage of curial members on councils and congregations ensures that the curia's views will have a strong voice at the meetings. In addition, since it is the curia that helps the pope screen and select candidates, vocal critics of the curia are not likely to be appointed."

the recent embarrassment caused with the Anglican Communion at the time of the publication of the papal document *Ad Tuendam Fidem*.[32] A commentary on this document signed by the Prefect and Secretary of the Congregation for the Doctrine of the Faith gave as an example of a definitive teaching to be held (*tenenda*) the declaration of Leo XIII in 1897 that Anglican orders are invalid.[33] In addition to being a surprise to most Catholic theologians of the world,[34] this statement was also a shock to the late Cardinal Basil Hume, Archbishop of Westminster[35] and to the Vatican President of the Council for the Promotion of Christian Unity. Published reports state that the Archbishop of Westminster had no previous knowledge of the decree and its commentary, and that he learned of it from the Archbishop of Canterbury. According to these same reports, the President of the Secretariat for Christian Unity, Cardinal Edward Cassidy, who was in England at the time to attend the Lambeth Conference of Bishops of the Anglican Communion as official representative of the Vatican, was informed only an hour before the commentary became public.[36] This would suggest that Cardinal Cassidy, in charge of the Vatican office for Christian unity, was not

---

[32] See full text in *Origins* 28, no. 8 (July 16, 1998): 113–16. The Latin title of the document means "to protect the faith."

[33] Cardinal Joseph Ratzinger and Archbishop Tarcisio Bertone, "Commentary on Profession of Faith's Concluding Paragraphs," *Origins* 28, no. 8 (July 16, 1998): 119. Some respected canonists hold that this commentary is not a document of the Congregation for the Doctrine of the Faith as such but a document of its authors, Cardinal Ratzinger and Archbishop Bertone, Prefect and Secretary of the congregation.

[34] See Francis A. Sullivan, S.J., "A New Obstacle to Anglican-Roman Catholic Dialogue," *America*, August 1–8, 1998, pp. 6–7.

[35] At the time of the reestablishment of the Catholic hierarchy in England (1850), it was agreed that Catholic dioceses would not take the name of Anglican dioceses in England. Consequently, since there is an Anglican bishop of London, the Catholic archbishop has the title Archbishop of Westminster.

[36] See "A Chill in the Atmosphere," *The Tablet,* July 11, 1998, p. 895.

consulted in the formation of the commentary. It is this kind of situation the council had in mind when it called for more coordination among the offices of the Curia. It is obvious what grave harm such an oversight can do to hopes for Christian unity.

Showing how generalized the lack of communication is, Thomas Reese reports:

> A group of American canonists visiting the curia were struck by how little communication there is between dicasteries. "They (i.e., the staff in the various Vatican offices) were curious to find out what we found out at other offices," explained a canonist. "It got so that we were bringing information that you would think would have gone by interdepartmental memo or something. There is more communication at my university than there is at this international headquarters. So it's very striking that they live in an isolated little world."[37]

3. Participation by Diocesan Bishops and Lay Persons

The Vatican II Decree on Bishops states: "It is also desirable that there should be co-opted into the membership of these departments [i.e., the Curia] some additional bishops, especially diocesan bishops, who are able to represent more fully to the supreme pontiff the mind, the aspirations and the needs of all the churches."[38] Note that the reason the council asked for the addition of diocesan bishops to curial offices is so that they may bring to the Pope the mind, the desires, and the hopes and needs of the different Churches. These bishops are not added to curial offices so that they can reflect the

---

[37] Reese, *Inside the Vatican*, 132.

[38] Decree on the Pastoral Office of Bishops in the Church §10, in *Decrees of the Ecumenical Councils,* ed. Tanner, 2:925. The Latin text of "It is desirable" is "*In votis quoque est.*" *In votis* conveys a stronger sense than "it is desirable," meaning there is a desire, a longing and a request for. See Charlton T. Lewis and Charles Short, *A Latin Dictionary* (New York: Oxford University Press, 1962), s.v. *votum*, p. 2015.

thinking of the Curia. They are to broaden the thinking of the Curia.

Speaking of lay persons, the council decrees: "Finally, the fathers of the council judge that it would be of great service for these departments to hear more often the view of lay people distinguished for virtue, knowledge and experience in order that they too may play an appropriate part in the affairs of the church."[39] These lay men and women are to be brought in precisely so that they can bring something new to the thinking and outlook of the Curia. They are not envisioned simply as a panel of mirrors exactly reflecting the mind and outlook of the Curia.

Diocesan bishops have indeed been added to both the councils and the congregations. But the vision of Vatican II has not been entirely realized. An American cardinal, for example, told me several years ago that he had never been invited to a meeting of the congregation of which he was a member. I was once appointed a consultor to a Vatican congregation for a five-year term. In that time I was consulted only by mail and not more than three times.

Lay persons have in fact been added to the membership of some councils, yet, thirty-five years after this decree of an ecumenical council, half the curial councils still have no lay men or women members.[40] Lay persons are not members of any of the congregations.[41] The council's hopes in regard to the participation by lay men and women in the Curia has not been fully realized. Women are significantly absent from major curial roles.

---

[39] *Decrees of the Ecumenical Councils,* ed. Tanner, 2:925.

[40] Reese, *Inside the Vatican,* 118. According to Reese, the difference between congregations and councils "has more to do with prestige and authority than with organizational structure."

[41] In the structure of the Curia there are congregations, councils, and tribunals. The councils came into existence as a result of Vatican II. They are such bodies as the Pontifical Council for the Family and the Pontifical Council for Justice and Peace. There are eleven councils and nine congretations. See Reese, *Inside the Vatican,* 112ff.

"Protectors" of the Church

All these things cumulatively support the belief that there is a continuity between the curial attitude of resistance at the time of Vatican II and curial policies today. Bishops, then and now, believe that there is among members of the Curia a certain proprietary sense over the Church and, to some degree, over the Pope. Is this pure imagination? Not entirely. At the time of Vatican II,

> [T]he general program of this group was "to prevent any lessening of papal prerogatives; to avoid reform of the Curia itself by the Council; to check the increase of bishops' powers; to resist the meddling of the laity; to moderate and apply gradually reforms of any kind." It considered itself "the remnant of Israel," that is, the minority that was the trustee and interpreter of God's will.[42]

Many bishops in all parts of the world would regard this description as an accurate picture of segments of the curia today.

Resistance to Vatican Council II

Another sign that this curial mind-set still exists is indicated by incidents such as those described above, but in a more observable way by what may be called the restorationist direction of the Curia at the present time. This seems to be an effort to recreate the preconciliar situation of the Church. It is manifest, for instance, in the encouragement of a return to the preconciliar Latin liturgy. This began as a limited concession with the hope of avoiding a schism on the part of the followers of Archbishop Marcel Lefebvre.[43] The concession did

---

[42] Alberigo and Komonchak, *History of Vatican II,* 2:109–10.

[43] Archbishop Lefebvre was a French Catholic archbishop who had been a member of Vatican II. He was leader of a movement that bitterly opposed the reforms of the liturgy at the council and sought to restore the use of the Latin liturgy as used prior to the council. The council itself had not forbidden the use of Latin in the liturgy as reformed by Vatican II. But

not in fact avoid schism, but it has led to the development of groups who rally around a return to the preconciliar liturgical forms. These groups now use not only the preconciliar Mass liturgy but also the preconciliar sacramental liturgies.[44] From being a concession granted as an extreme measure to avoid schism, the return to the preconciliar liturgy has now become almost a campaign.

Cardinal Ratzinger, for instance, holder of one of the most important and influential offices in the Vatican Curia, was quoted in an interview as saying:

> On the basis of my experience, I am convinced above all that we must do everything possible to form a new generation of prelates who can see that this is not an attack on the Council . . . we must . . . help priests and bishops of goodwill to see that celebrating the liturgy according to the old texts does not mean overshadowing.[45]

This would seem to be a statement that the Curia has the role of teaching and shaping the episcopate on a matter that

---

the Pope did suppress the use of the Latin rite of the Mass as it existed prior to the council so that those who wished to use Latin should use the reformed rite of the Mass.

[44] This ranging beyond the Latin Mass reformed by the Council of Trent to the Tridentine form of the sacraments is surprising. After all, Pope Paul VI, by an act of the supreme apostolic authority, changed the form of several of the sacraments. Is another act of the supreme apostolic authority necessary to change the form of the sacraments back? Has this been done? Furthermore, the entire liturgical reform of the council was made on the basis of significant theological principles, among them giving new emphasis to the centrality of the mystery of Christ and opening this mystery more effectively to the people. The reform was not a superficial matter of introducing the vernacular or changing ritual. Can these theological principles now be simply set aside? What is to be said of the RCIA (Rite of Christian Initiation of Adults)? Is this required of those who return to the past forms? If not, how does such a return to the past respond to the deep theological and patristic developments which underlie a thing such as the RCIA?

[45] Remarks of Cardinal Joseph Ratzinger in *30 Days*, no. 11 (1998): 46.

is not of faith. The assumption of such a role by the Curia seems to be quite in conflict with the understanding of the episcopate as taught in Vatican II and as taught in the divine tradition of the Church. The episcopate is not simply a secondary body to be shaped and formed to a certain point of view by the Curia, especially on matters open to free opinion in the Church. Admittedly the Curia has delegated authority. It is quite another thing when the Curia assumes a role of authority over the episcopate to shape its thinking in a matter open to legitimate debate in the Church. Not only has the cardinal expressed this need to form a new kind of bishop who will favor the preconciliar liturgy, but he himself at times publicly celebrates the liturgy in this form.[46] For such an influential and central figure of the Vatican to invest himself in word and action to such a high degree in promoting the preconciliar liturgy and to declare that the Curia must form bishops who will follow his lead is a matter of great significance.

In the same vein, while collegiality was a major feature of Vatican II, numerous curial decisions have been made that run counter to it. Repeatedly decisions of episcopal conferences—whose creation was strongly urged by the council—have been rescinded. Translations of the Catechism and of the Lectionary that have been approved by conferences in various countries have been rejected by the Curia. A plan for the working relationship of bishops with Catholic universities

---

[46] Catholic News Service published an article concerning Cardinal Ratzinger celebrating the preconciliar liturgy entitled "Celebrates Tridentine Mass." The article appeared in various Catholic papers, and I cite it from the *Catholic San Francisco,* April 30, 1999. This article incorrectly states that Cardinal Ratzinger said that Pope Paul VI's Mass reforms provoked extremely serious damage. What the cardinal did say, however, is that Paul VI's *suppression* of the preconciliar liturgy caused "extremely serious damage" and this suppression marked "a break in the history of the liturgy, the consequences of which could only be tragic." The article goes on to report that the cardinal believes that there are good reasons to turn the altar back facing the wall as in the past.

and colleges that was approved by the American episcopal conference by a vote of 224 to 6 was rejected. In the appointment of bishops, it is not uncommon for bishops to be named who have never been proposed by the bishops of a region and are even unknown to them.

Commentators, therefore, cannot be faulted who believe, that in the aggregate, such things amount to a restorationist policy very much in line with the curial bloc of Vatican II which opposed the Council. What has been said in this chapter alone would seem to bear out that there still exists the determination to "check the increase of bishops' powers; to resist the meddling of the laity; to moderate and apply gradually reforms of any kind."[47]

In light of these things, there is a certain familiar note in the statement that for the curial bloc at Vatican II, "the greatest of errors . . . was the claim of episcopal collegiality, which they saw as an attack on the Curia."[48] Nor is it entirely unfounded to believe that this sentiment survives in some segments of the Curia today.

While all these things constitute a discernible and serious problem, past and present, it would be incorrect to portray everyone in the Curia as belonging to this mind-set. The Curia is not a homogeneous mass. Some members of the Curia, at all levels, are clearly aware of the needs and the problems of the Church and recognize what an obstacle to the mission of the Church and to Christian unity some present policies and modes of behavior are.

Nor should these observations be read to imply that those who are participants in the restorationist or resistance blocs in the Curia are insincere or lacking in true love and devotion to the Church. But despite the good intentions that underlie them, there is widespread conviction that these policies are destructive and counterproductive to the goal of Christian

---

[47] See Alberigo and Komonchak, *History of Vatican II,* 2:109–10.
[48] Ibid., 2:210.

unity, and that is the point that must be more openly dealt with.[49]

Ideas for Curial Reform at Vatican II

During discussions at the time of Vatican II, several specific proposals were made for a reform of the curia.

1. An Overall Congregation

The archbishop of Florence proposed creating an overall congregation that would include some diocesan bishops from various countries. This overall congregation would have authority over all the rest of the Curia and would promote the proper coordination among the other congregations. This reflects the system of the consistory prior to the late sixteenth century.[50]

2. Fewer Bishops and Priests

The German Cardinal Frings proposed that there should be fewer bishops and priests in the Curia and more lay persons.[51] While some proposed greater internationalization of the Curia, the Italian Cardinal Lercaro and the African Cardinal Rugambwa rightly pointed out that the problems of curial reform would not be solved simply by internationalization of the membership. This observation has been verified in the more than thirty years since the council.

---

[49] Holiness and goodness do not guarantee the prudence of contingent policy decisions. For instance, one may certainly question whether the methods used by St. Pius X to oppose modernism were prudent.

[50] See Mörsdorf, "Decree," 173–75.

[51] Ibid., 174: "As regards the officials in the Roman Curia, Cardinal Frings asked that fewer bishops and priests and more laymen should be employed. No one was consecrated a bishop only to honour his person or office, for being a bishop was itself an office, not an honour to be added to another office."

3. "Two Curias"

Some bishops at Vatican II proposed that it would be necessary to distinguish between the Pope's two roles: the role of the universal primacy and the more limited role Patriarch of the West.[52] In light of this distinction they proposed that there should be two Curias, one for the universal Church and one for the Latin Churches of the West.

Some Present Possibilities for Reform

1. Fewer Bishops and More Lay Persons in the Curia

A reform of the Curia might begin with the recommendation of Cardinal Frings at Vatican II that there be fewer bishops and priests in the Curia. This goal has to be pursued keeping in mind the call of the council that some bishops should be members of curial departments. The recommendation, then, of fewer bishops in the Curia would mean in reality just that. It would mean not absolutely eliminating them but reducing their number. There is a great potential advantage in having as members of the Curia some who have had the experience of being diocesan bishops, provided they contribute a fresh outlook deriving from their experience and do not merely reflect curial ways of thinking. In regard to bishops in the Curia, some are resident in Rome and serve in the curial departments. Others remain in their dioceses and attend meetings at stated intervals in Rome. It is the number of *in curia* bishops that especially needs consideration.

Bishops holding office in the Curia are generally either prefects or secretaries of Vatican departments. The prefect is in charge of the department, the secretary is the second in command. The number of bishops, almost always cardinals, who are heads of departments could be reduced. There does not seem to be any compelling reason why a bishop must be head of the department dealing with the laity, with culture, with

---

[52] Ibid.

Catholic education, with communications, with family life, or with several others.

Many believe that the problem is more acute when it comes to the secretaries of the Vatican departments. Increasingly there are those who see the ordination of a priest as bishop in order to be secretary of a curial congregation as an abuse of the sacrament of Holy Orders and of the office of bishop. This practice has the appearance of making a priest a bishop in order to give him rank or prestige. It is also an ecumenical problem because it appears to quarrel with the teaching of the Church about the episcopate.[53] A second reason to diminish the presence of cardinals and bishops in the Curia is that such a move would be a sign that the Curia, though possessing delegated papal authority, is not a *tertium quid,* subordinate to the Pope but superior to the episcopate.

The diminishment of the numbers of cardinals and bishops in the Curia would also be a way of opening more curial responsibilities to lay men and women. This is what is happening in diocesan curias, where lay persons are assuming responsibilities once held only by priests.

2. *Limited Terms*

A practical measure that could also contribute to a reform of curial policies would be limited terms for Curia members.[54] One reason is that at present members of the Curia may span

---

[53] At the present time, in addition to prefects and secretaries of congregations, the papal master of ceremonies and the head of the papal household are bishops. Objections to this practice cannot be read to infer that these bishops lack the qualifications to be a bishop. The question centers on the propriety of making priests bishops in order to hold such roles.

[54] The heads of curial departments are appointed for a five-year term. But in some instances their appointment is renewed and even renewed three or four times. Some curial personnel do not belong to the Curia as such. These usually serve there for six years or so and then return permanently to their home country. Other personnel who do belong to the Curia may stay on for many years.

several pontificates. Proprietary instincts and the feeling of having all the answers are nourished by extended tenure. This is a major problem. On the one hand, it would be impossible to have a Curia that was constantly changing and had no institutional memory. It would be harmful to the unity of the Church if such were the case and would be of little help to the Pope. But a way must be found to retain the necessary benefits of continuity with the equally necessary benefits of fresh approaches.

Given the fact that the term for curial officials is now five years, a helpful move might be the creation of a policy that a curial official, after serving at most two terms, would have to leave curial service for a time before being eligible to return to it. As a rule, if the person is going to return to the Curia, he or she should be required to take a sabbatical, preferably in the home country and become involved in the life of the local church. Such a return to the actual lived situation of the Church could help to broaden and refine the valuable, more universal perspective one's curial service can give. In the case of certain very sensitive functions which have been discharged with great effectiveness—such as, for example, in the Secretariat of State, which has dealings with very complex issues around the world, or in the Vatican councils, which deal with Christian unity where much depends on personal contacts and personal trust—there could be provision for exceptions.

It could also be beneficial if all curial officials were required to attend a certain number of seminars or workshops on a variety of issues each year. To be truly beneficial such seminars would have to include viewpoints not necessarily approved of by the Curia. Participation in these seminars should not be taken as a sign of agreement with everything presented.[55] But the challenge of probing, listen-

---

[55] Listening to presenters with differing points of view which does not of itself mean agreement with those points of view has some analogies with the diplomatic practice of the Holy See. Pope John Paul II, addressing the diplomatic corps on October 20, 1978, pointed out: "Diplomatic

ing, and responding to new ideas and approaches is in itself broadening and enriching. It can also deepen faith by forcing the process of clarification.

3. The Process of Selecting Candidates for the Roman Curia

An important aspect of any reform of the Curia is the selection of those chosen to serve there. Bishops are sometimes asked to release a priest for service in the Curia, but they are not asked their opinion about his qualifications for such a post or about how he has fulfilled his responsibilities in the diocese. Members of religious orders have been chosen for curial service against the decision of their major superiors. Such policies are obviously in conflict with the canons of the most ordinary prudence.

Some priests desire posts in the Curia because they do not like pastoral work—if they have ever engaged in it—or because they ambition higher things and regard the Curia as a stepping stone, or because they think there is a certain glamor and prestige attaching to curial service. It is probably impossible to exclude all such types, but effort should be made to ascertain a candidate's motives and attitude toward curial service. Anyone who has had more than superficial contact with the Curia knows that there are also many truly spiritual priests who serve in the Curia out of a deep faith and in response to an invitation that they did not seek. But selection policies are critical.

A very important factor for selecting priests or bishops for curial service is how the general body of the priests in their diocese or the bishops in their country regard them. Certainly it is not a popularity contest. But when a priest or bishop has

---

relations . . . do not necessarily manifest, on my side, approval of such and such a regime . . . . Obviously, neither do they manifest approval of all its acts in the conduct of public affairs." See *L'Osservatore Romano,* English edition, November 2, 1978, no. 44, p. 3.

the genuine respect of his peers, this is a good indication of his character. When nurses and doctors have high regard for another doctor, it is a good sign that he or she is accomplished and has a degree of excellence in the profession.

The overall goal of curial reform is decentralization, subsidiarity, and collegiality. It will therefore be necessary to select those who understand and support these aims and have the qualities to work in such a context and with such a spirit.

4. A Commission for the Reform of the Curia

Obviously, to reform the Curia in a way that is needed by the Church for the future is an immense undertaking that is both complex and delicate. No single person is capable of such a task.

There is much more to consider than the few ideas and suggestions raised in this chapter. One way, then, of pursuing curial reform would be for the Pope to create a commission headed by three presidents: the president of an episcopal conference, a lay person, and a representative of the Curia.[56] Noting that the importance of a major reform of the Curia cannot be overestimated, I proposed on another occasion:

> Under this three-member presidency, there could be a working commission which would include bishops, priests, religious and lay persons. The commission should be given a timeline of not more than three years and should have authority to consult experts in management, government, theology, canon law and other useful disciplines and professions.[57] The Pope and the episcopal conferences should be kept informed of the progress of the work. When it is completed and in a state which the Pope indicates he could accept, the plan should be presented for a vote to the presidents of episcopal conferences in a meeting held for this pur-

---

[56] See my lecture "The Exercise of the Primacy," *Commonweal* 123, no. 13 (July 12, 1996): 14–15.

[57] To this list of fields of expertise I would add experts in church history.

pose and presented to the Pope for his formal approval and implementation. At this time the Pope in consultation with the episcopal conferences could create an implementation commission to oversee the carrying out of the restructuring and with the mandate to report to the Pope periodically. The work of the commission should be public and its conclusions should be public.[58]

The reform of the Curia, notwithstanding the Curia's indispensable role of service to the Pope and the fact that it has brought many benefits to the Church at large, is perhaps in the end the single most important factor in the serious pursuit of Christian unity and in responding to the Pope's aim of finding a new way of exercising the primacy "open to the new situation." It is imperative to recognize that all hope for Christian unity cannot be pinned only on the theological dialogues.

---

[58] Quinn, "Exercise of the Primacy," 14.

Conclusion

Coming now to the end of this response to Pope John Paul's invitation to dialogue about the primacy, I acknowledge the limited character of what I have written. No doubt other topics should be introduced, and about those which I have discussed here, more should perhaps have been said. I have rarely given a talk, a homily, or written an article without someone pointing out that I failed to speak about something of great concern to them. Recently, for instance, when I gave a talk about collegiality, someone asked why I had not mentioned the real presence of Christ in the Eucharist. Ronald Knox once said, "It is not necessary to say everything in order to say something." My goal in this book has not been to say everything but to make a beginning, to say something. It is one bishop's initial effort at a response.

All that I have been able to deal with here, however, leads me to believe that in the exercise of the papacy two things, more than others, are the greatest problem for the Church and for Christian unity. The first is centralization; the other, the need for reform of the Roman Curia.

The question of centralization is encountered at the theological level in the doctrine of collegiality and communion. Theologically there seems to be a contradiction in the minute and growing centralization on the part of Rome, on the one hand, and the teaching of the Church about collegiality and communion, on the other. There is a similar contradiction between the genuine and courageous call for Christian unity and the insistence on and expansion of centralization, with its resultant abridgment of collegiality and legitimate diversity.

At the practical level, centralization to the degree that it now exists presents a growing and impossible task in a world Church of such diversity and in an age of instant communication and rapid change. One commentator has stated that the present condition of Roman centralization is near the point of implosion.

There is a striking parallel between the need for decentralization in the Church and the experience of international corporations, of the International Red Cross, and of various organizations of the United Nations. Large international corporations, for example, have discovered that too much centralized control is counterproductive. Many of them have adopted the formula of "directed autonomy."[1] It is described this way:

> In directed autonomy, people in every nook and cranny of the company are empowered—encouraged, in fact—to do things their way. Suggestions are actively sought. But this all takes place within a context of direction. People know what the boundaries are; they know where they should act on their own and where not. The boss knows that his or her job is to establish those boundaries, then truly get out of the way.[2]

A major difficulty in big corporations that try to implement directed autonomy is the resistance of second-level managers. "A continuing problem . . . is the unwillingness of old-school managers to refrain from being secretive and directive. To them employee involvement feels like loss of control."[3]

The Church, of course, is not an international corporation, nor, on the other hand, does it live a timeless, transcen-

---

[1] For an extensive treatment of the imperative of decentralization and yet control and coordination in international corporations, see Robert H. Waterman, Jr., *The Renewal Factor* (New York: Bantam Books, 1987).

[2] Ibid., 75.

[3] Ibid., 86.

dent existence. The Church is both affected by and can learn from the world and in particular from the experience of international corporations or the United Nations or the Red Cross. Directed autonomy simply shows how secular corporations that are international, multicultural, and dealing with complex, diverse, and swiftly changing situations have learned an effective way of avoiding obsolescence, chaos, and fragmentation. Directed autonomy in international corporations can offer some suggestions to the Church to help it to learn how, in the practical realm, it can decentralize, encourage diversity, elicit participation, and implement the principle of subsidiarity and the doctrine of effective collegiality without running the risk of chaos or of schismatic or national churches.

It shows how legitimate and creative diversity can really be an antidote to centrifugal independence. Legitimate diversity and creativity will bring with them the need for coordination and the need for accountability. If in the thirteenth century Thomas could illuminate divine revelation through co-opting the systems and categories of pagan philosophers, surely it is not heterodox for the Church of the third millennium to consider how the categories and structures of international corporations could be adapted to serve diversity within communion and unity.

Once the decision is made to move toward decentralization, the substantial reform of the Roman Curia will be inevitable. At the same time, decentralization will only serve to make the Curia more important as a means of coordination, of information gathering and sharing, in support of collegial, directed autonomy. If the curia does not change, and decentralization does not take place, there will ensue great disorder in the Church because of its inability to respond to changing situations with sufficient rapidity, and the inability of an omnicompetent central bureaucracy to have an adequate grasp of swiftly changing, multicultural situations. It will be the paradox of the insistence on central control being, in reality, the loss of control.

It is immensely significant that in Orthodox, Anglican, or Protestant dialogues about Christian unity there is no mention of abolishing the papacy as a condition for unity. There is, in fact, a growing realization of the true service the Petrine ministry offers the whole Church, how truly providential the primacy is. A major example of the importance of the primacy is the Second Vatican Council. It did not come about because of a great groundswell among the people, priests, or bishops of the world. It was the result of a papal initiative. Without the council it is anyone's guess where the Catholic Church might be at this time. Without the council it is likely that there would never have been an encyclical like *Ut unum sint*. The combination of this growing openness and the Pope's prophetic call to probe the primacy is one of those unique moments in history. If there is too much delay, too much diffidence, the time will pass. It is imperative not to lose this moment of grace.

Now the question is: When will the Catholic bishops of the world and their conferences take up the dialogue about the exercise of the primacy raised in *Ut unum sint* with the honesty and seriousness it deserves?

Epilogue

The greatest corrective to centralization in Rome will occur the day a Protestant church comes knocking on the Vatican door to say: "We want corporate union." Over and over again church leaders have said that they hope and pray for unity, but it will be fascinating when someone finally calls the cards so that they have to do something about a concrete bid. Then it will no longer be possible to postpone until the distant future the question of how the Papacy would have to function in a united Church. . . . Such a daring request for corporate union might be the ultimate challenge to the successor of Peter, testing what it means to feed the sheep of Jesus. . . .

It has been the Papacy's proudest boast that to Peter alone among all the disciples Jesus gave the power of the keys. A Protestant church asking for corporate union would be asking Peter's successor to use those keys to get the door open.

—Raymond E. Brown, *Crises Facing the Church* (New York: Paulist Press, 1975), 83.

Index

OF RELATED INTEREST

Phyllis Zagano & Terrence W. Tilley, Editors

THE EXERCISE OF THE PRIMACY
Continuing the Dialogue

*Archbishop Quinn's remarkable Oxford lecture
on the relationship between the Pope and the bishops
with responses by leading scholars.*

In June, 1996, **Archbishop John Quinn** delivered a lecture
at Campion Hall at Oxford on the relationship between the
Pope and the bishops, offering both an acute assessment of
the present situation and bold proposals for reform.
In order to carry forward the discussion occasioned
by Archbishop Quinn's lecture, this volume presents
the text of the Oxford lecture as well as responses
by five prominent Catholic thinkers who examine
the issues raised from a variety of perspectives:

**R. Scott Appleby
Elizabeth A. Johnson
John F. Kane
Thomas P. Rausch
Wendy M. Wright.**

0-8245-1744-x; $14.95 paperback

---

*At your bookstore or, to order directly from the publisher,
please send check or money order (including $3.00
for the first book plus $1.00 for each additional book) to:*

THE CROSSROAD PUBLISHING COMPANY
370 LEXINGTON AVENUE, NEW YORK, NY 10017

We hope you enjoyed The Reform of the Papacy.
Thank you for reading it.

herder & herder